BONSAI
MINIATURE TREES

BONSAI
MINIATURE TREES

by CLAUDE CHIDAMIAN

WITH ILLUSTRATIONS BY
SHIRLEA HATCHER

D. VAN NOSTRAND COMPANY
PRINCETON, NEW JERSEY
TORONTO · LONDON
NEW YORK

To
P. B. P.

Preface

PERHAPS THE GREATEST obstacle I have encountered in twenty years of studying and growing bonsai has been the lack of a single good book in English on the subject. Occasional articles in garden magazines and brief notes in horticultural encyclopedias have offered little help. Even the recent appearance of several small books on bonsai has proved a disappointment. Norio Kobayashi's *Bonsai— Miniature Potted Trees* (Tokyo, Japan Travel Bureau, 1950), Alfred Koehn's *Notes on Bonsai* (Tokyo, Foreign Affairs Association of Japan, 1952), and the Brooklyn Botanic Garden's *Handbook on Dwarfed Potted Trees* (Brooklyn, New York, 1953), although well illustrated and written by experts, are all too brief and set in English that is more often quaint than clear.

Of the numerous pamphlets, catalogs, and brochures published by mail-order bonsai promoters revealing "ancient expert's secrets," the less said the better. The truth of the matter is simply this—no one reading the material on bonsai available in English today could possibly make a good bonsai, let alone understand its true meaning.

But criticism is easy, performance difficult. After I began this book I understood why it had not been written before —why it must perhaps be written again by others in years to come. For bonsai are far more than potted plants, they are works of art. The author writing on them might as easily explain how to compose a fine symphony, paint a master-piece, or write great literature.

The mechanical aspects of bonsai are simple enough to explain. There is no magic in bonsai culture. Its techniques are based on sound horticultural principles, experience, and patience. But the artistic side of these tiny trees is well-nigh impossible to convey. Bonsai are planted in philosophy, shaped by art, grown with love. Without some grasp of this intangible artistic process, the bare technique of making bonsai amounts to nothing.

If this book succeeds in bringing this feeling and appre-ciation for bonsai to the reader, it may deserve to be the first complete book on the subject in English.

CLAUDE CHIDAMIAN

Los Angeles
July 1955

Table of Contents

List of Illustrations

(Courtesy of Brooklyn Botanic Garden)

List of Illustrations

BONSAI
MINIATURE TREES

What Are Bonsai?

CHAPTER I   *F*OR at least ten centuries the Japanese have cultivated the dwarf potted trees called bonsai. A tiny dish, a handful of soil, a living plant have been for all that time the unique art of a people whose "great genius lies in little things."

But now, quite suddenly, Western gardeners have discovered the rare beauty and charm of these miniature plants. Perhaps this new interest started with our imitation "Ming Trees," those ever-popular landscapes made of dry twigs and dyed moss seen in every florist's shop. Or perhaps it was returning servicemen who brought tales from Japan of real dwarfed trees, centuries old, actually growing in tiny pots. No matter how it began, bonsai are making a brilliant debut today in American flower shows, nurseries, homes, and gardens. And it is no wonder.

When you see a little tree one foot high that seems a hundred, when you know it's ten years old but it looks a thousand, when you can fairly hear the birds singing in its

1

tiny boughs—that's magic. But in Japan, where this sort of thing has been going on for centuries, they simply call it bonsai. But *bonsai* or *magic,* it takes sleight of hand to create these miniature potted trees and an optical illusion to enjoy them. Here's how it's done.

From gardens, fields, and mountains, from the wind-swept crags above the sea, plants for bonsai are carefully chosen. Pines, juniper, maple, and many more—naturally dwarfed plants gnarled and twisted by weather and privation—they are skillfully dug and their roots pruned and prepared for shallow pots scarcely large enough to hold them. Choosing the right containers for bonsai is as important as selecting the right plants, for they are traditionally grown in small ceramic trays, pans, or dishes of many sizes, shapes, and colors.

Once the plant and container have been chosen the bonsai is firmly potted, thoroughly watered, and carefully sheltered until it becomes reestablished. Many plants are lost in the process, some hopelessly weakened, others spoiled.

Actually few of the trees or shrubs collected are so well shaped that they need not be trimmed and trained before they can make good bonsai. And it is this technique that makes bonsai culture an art. It is difficult to describe the skill and sensitivity of the master artisan as the plants come to life at his touch.

By carefully pruning some branches, by tying and bending others, he gradually gives his tiny tree an ancient, weathered look. And if he is truly successful, he will create a strange illusion. The little tree will be so perfectly proportioned in every leaf, twig, and branch, its roots and trunk so realistically gnarled and twisted that anyone who sees it will forget that it is only a miniature. He will feel as if he is actually standing before a giant of the forest.

That's the magic of bonsai. Using the highest skills of the gardener, the eye of a painter, the touch of a sculptor, the bonsai maker perfectly recreates a scene from nature that can be held in the palm of one's hand. For bonsai are not simply potted plants to be appreciated for their beautiful foliage and flowers, but works of art as suggestive and appealing as sculpture, poetry, and painting. In them we can visualize the grandeur of great forest trees twisted and bent by storms and age, relive the wonder of distant places, or see the restless seasons change before our eyes.

The poet Buson captured this magic quality of bonsai when he wrote,

> Granted this dew-drop world is but
> A dew-drop world—this granted, yet. . .

It is no wonder that the artistic, impressionable Japanese have treasured these miniatures for centuries.

BONSAI IN THE EAST

Although the Japanese perfected the art of dwarfed trees, they did not invent it. As with so much else in Japanese culture, the idea of bonsai was borrowed intact from China.

In the Chinese Lunar New Year, with its timeless symbolism and pageantry, we find the real origin of bonsai. For countless ages the Chinese have grown the flowering peach, apricot, meratia, and forsythia—nature's own harbingers of spring and life—to decorate their most joyous festival. The potted plants carefully grown in paper-screened houses, pruned and wired in grotesque shapes, were forced into bloom to welcome the New Year.

The Japanese no doubt first borrowed this idea for their own New Year celebrations. Tiny pots containing a flowering apricot, a few sprigs of bamboo, and a little gnarled pine still decorate almost every home in the New Year season, bringing good luck and long life to the household. But in time this seasonal custom merged with two other ideas borrowed from China—first, the Chinese use of potted flowering and fruiting trees to decorate their secluded courtyards; and second, the Chinese rockery, made by piling up stones and slabs of rock into grotesque shapes to represent distant mountain scenery.

At some time—no one knows when—these three ideas fused. The little potted New Year tree was cultivated to decorate both home and garden the year round. Its grotesque shape was studied and refined. A few stones and bits of moss were added to the pot, and the distant mountain scene so crudely suggested in the Chinese rockery suddenly came to life.

The first authentic record of bonsai is found in a celebrated picture scroll, or *emakimono*, dated 1310. Here are pictured not only miracles of the Kasuga shrine at Nara and great moments from the life of Honen Shonin, founder of the Jodo sect of Buddhism, but dwarfed trees and grasses growing in shallow pots as garden ornaments.

Through the long years of civil war in medieval Japan the idea of bonsai slowly took root in the common man and great hero alike. In the fifteenth century we encounter a reference to bonsai in the classic Noh play *Hachi-no-Ki*, or *The Potted Trees*. The quietly moving drama tells of Sano Genzaemon, an impoverished but warm-hearted samurai, who burns his favorite bonsai to warm a guest on a cold

HOW BONSAI DEVELOPED

1. The Chinese Lunar New Year, with its flowering trees and symbolism, was the real origin of bonsai.

2. The potted flowers and fruits of Chinese courtyards and gardens were an important influence too.

3. The Chinese rockery, representing distant mountain scenes, influenced bonsai as well as Japanese landscaping.

4. From the flowering apricot, bamboo, and pine that decorate the Japanese New Year feast, bonsai gradually evolved.

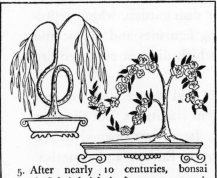

5. After nearly 10 centuries, bonsai reached their height in the grotesque specimens of the Tokugawa Era.

6. Today bonsai are achieving a new popularity with more natural forms, wider appeal, and greater usefulness.

5

wintry night, a guest who proves to be a great shogun traveling in disguise.

The audiences who applauded that drama had already begun to appreciate a more peaceful way of life, and succeeding years saw the cults of bonsai, flower arrangement, and tea ceremony spread throughout the land. With the coming of the Tokugawa Era—those 250 years of isolation and peace through the seventeenth, eighteenth, and nineteenth centuries—bonsai flourished with all the arts, becoming more refined and elaborate, more a part of traditional Japanese culture than ever before.

Near the end of this time, a little more than a hundred years ago, the word *bonsai* itself first came into use. For centuries the little trees had been called *hachi-no-ki,* "trees in pots," as in the old Noh play. But as the cult reached its height in the nineteenth century, its followers wanted some exclusive term to distinguish their works of art from common potted plants. So they borrowed again, using two Chinese characters, *p'ên tsai,* meaning "planted in a shallow vessel," which they pronounced *bone-sigh.*

Now the little magic trees were set apart from all the other forms of potted plants: the *hachi-ue,* or ordinary potted plant; the *hachi-niwa,* or dish garden, which reproduced a landscape literally using figurines and props; and the *bonkei,* or tray landscape, which did not even require live plants in its make-up.

Now the bonsai cult felt safe and secure with its new name, inflexible rules, and ancient traditions. But the next year the Tokugawa Era ended, Japan was opened to the world, and bonsai found its way to Europe and America.

BONSAI IN THE WEST

The first Westerners who explored newly opened Japan were amazed and delighted with the art of bonsai. Chief among these was Philipp Franz von Siebold, who even earlier had managed to live for a while in the hermit kingdom as an emissary of the Dutch East India Company. In his *Flora Japonica* he wrote:

> The Japanese have an incredible fondness for dwarf trees, and with reference to this the cultivation of the Ume, or Plum, is one of the most general and lucrative employments of the country. Such plants are increased by in-arching, and by this means specimens are obtained which have the peculiar habit of the Weeping Willow. A nurseryman offered me for sale in 1826 a plant in flower which was scarcely three inches high; this *chef d'oeuvre* of gardening was grown in a little lacquered box of three tiers, similar to those filled with drugs which the Japanese carry in their belts; in the upper tier was this Ume, in the second row a little Spruce Fir, and at the lowest a Bamboo scarcely an inch and a half high.

The newcomers perhaps did not always see bonsai as works of art. But as incredible curiosities from an unbelievable land they carried them off in great numbers to Europe and America. Without the patient care and love of their creators, these first bonsai withered in stuffy Victorian drawing rooms and conservatories, for no one in all the world really knew how to care for them but the Japanese. Soon stories began to circulate about these magical little trees. Their culture was pronounced one of the great mysteries of the Orient. Tall tales and fabulous legends grew up about bonsai—myths that still persist today.

Open almost any garden magazine and you will see the

"Living Ming Tree" advertisements. Unscrupulous promoters offer all the "secrets" of growing dwarfed trees and a package of special seed guaranteed to produce real bonsai for a not so modest sum. The very fact that these advertisements run year after year proves that the "Big Lie" about bonsai is still very much alive; but more important still, it proves that Western gardeners have a genuine interest in bonsai that must be met honestly.

For many years Japanese in America and Europe have imported bonsai from Japan or raised excellent specimens of their own. But until very recently their efforts were a labor of love, scarcely shared by their neighbors. In modern Japan the bonsai cult, now simplified, Westernized, and democratized, flourishes as strong as ever. Bonsai clubs, schools, magazines, and shows are found everywhere. But here in America we have only begun to meet the rising interest in bonsai.

A dozen excellent bonsai nurseries in California, a thriving club in Southern California, splendid displays of bonsai in flower shows, and bonsai collections in public places as the Brooklyn Botanic Garden in New York is a good beginning. But it is only a beginning. There are still those who think bonsai are only for the Japanese, who believe there are real "secrets" in bonsai culture, who have never experienced the magic of these tiny trees. This book is for them.

The Magic of Bonsai

CHAPTER II   *T H E* magic of bonsai lies in the spirit and culture of the people of Japan themselves. Nowhere on earth have men lived so close to nature, worshipped its deities in ancient times and celebrated its beauties with festival, song, and story in the present. And nowhere else on earth has nature shown such bewildering variety and awesome majesty to capture the heart of man.

Is it any wonder that the Japanese have sought to hold fast to this never-ending source of inspiration, tried to picture its sublimity in their art, its simplicity in their flower arrangement, its vastness in their miniature potted trees? Is it any wonder that they place these objects in the *tokonoma,* or household altar, and kneel before them daily in contemplation?

It is this religious and philosophical aspect that gives bonsai its true meaning and worth, yet is so often overlooked or misunderstood. It is this same element of nature

9

worship that makes it so difficult for us to appreciate Japanese gardens. For the Japanese ideal of garden making is not to create a pleasant retreat or background for a home, but like bonsai to reproduce for intimate enjoyment the loftiest aspects of nature—distant natural scenes not otherwise available for daily contemplation. Scenes of wild and rugged splendor to stir the imagination and make the observer experience again the awe and reverence he felt when last he stood in that distant place. Understanding this we can never again see the Japanese garden as a beautiful toy-like miniature or define bonsai simply as a "dwarf potted tree." For the Japanese "finds tongues in trees, books in the running brooks, sermons in stones. . . ."

It is impossible to sum up the Japanese spirit in a single phrase, but if we remember that these people are largely Buddhist in philosophy, we can readily understand their underlying belief in a mystical consciousness of Life embodied in an Idea—here the Idea of growing things—coupled with a mystical confidence in all lesser life to express the greater. As men think, so they do—especially in making gardens. For every man's faith—or lack of it—is inevitably reflected in the garden he makes.

MUCH IN LITTLE

There is another facet to the Japanese character that must be understood if we are to appreciate bonsai fully. It is their great genius for doing little things.

Living Spartan-like in their tiny island kingdom, long isolated from the world, they have developed an uncanny faculty for making much of little. And herein lies both their greatness and weakness. For these people seem unable to produce anything of large scale and great substance, but rather excel in work requiring delicate skill and scrupulous execution. The deft hands that manipulate chopsticks and writing brush are wonderfully fitted to the miniature arts.

On a tiny button, or *netsuke,* Japanese artists of the To-kugawa Era lavished miracles of miniature sculpture such as the world has never known. Pieces of wood and ivory scarcely more than an inch in length came to life teeming with figures of men and gods, birds and beasts, breathing with impossible realism. And all this because traditional Japanese garments had no pockets and it was necessary to carry money, medicine, and tobacco in a pouch or case tied to the girdle by a cord at the end of which was the *netsuke.*

Even in poetry the Japanese have created a miniature form beside which our fourteen-line sonnet seems crude and overlong. The *haiku* with its seventeen syllables can express poetic feelings rarely touched in Western literature. Here, for example, the eighteenth-century poetess Kaga no Chiyo mourns her dead child,

> To-day, how far may he have wandered,
> The brave hunter of dragon flies?

The sublimity of those lines lies not in what they say, but what they suggest. A stone is cast in the pool of conscious-ness and the waves of connotation break on our minds and hearts in never-ending circles. We bring as much to the poem as the poet herself. We too become creators. It is the magic of bonsai all over again. It is the Japanese gift of cre-ating worlds in miniature.

THE VALUE OF BONSAI

Time and again in Japan one may see a moving van piled high with household goods and, riding at the very top, a little collection of bonsai. The plants may not be worth a dollar, but the proud owner will tell you how he collected that little pine in Shikoku, how he has lovingly tended the scarlet maple for thirty years. And quite suddenly we know these plants are priceless.

The value of bonsai cannot be measured in dollars, though some have sold for a thousand or more, but in the enduring beauty and interest they bring the grower. Many have learned the meaning of patience in the five, ten, or twenty years it takes to make a worthy tree. Many have discovered humility in studying the infinite complexity of a single leaf. Many have found peace in the quiet rhythm of the changing seasons.

It is not what we do to these plants that is important, but what they do to us. The need for patience, humility, and peace is universal. So too is the power of bonsai. It can touch alike the heart of an impoverished fifteenth-century Japanese samurai or calm the troubled mind of the twentieth-century American. Even you and I can find a greater measure of faith, courage, and understanding living and growing with bonsai.

Bonsai in the Home and Garden

CHAPTER III   *T*H E Japanese have long used
bonsai to decorate their homes
and gardens. Although they cannot be grown as house
plants, bonsai are often brought in for a day to be displayed
in the *tokonoma* or alcove that is a prominent feature in
every Japanese home. Here on a small pedestal, with perhaps a scroll painting hanging behind it, the bonsai works
its magic. A little tree scarcely a foot high seems to reach
the clouds. A piece of stone suggests Mt. Fuji; a drop of
water, the glistening sea. Perspectives change, tensions vanish, we feel a strange repose.

Much of the effectiveness of bonsai in the Japanese home
lies in the quality of the house itself. Nowhere on earth have
architects achieved such pure beauty and simplicity as in
the traditional Japanese home. Just as we must take off our
street shoes to enter it, so we must leave behind all our
garish Western ideas and gadgets to appreciate it. Here is
beauty achieved by quiet thought, by selection and elimina-

tion, by stripping every human requirement to its essentials.
There are no pictures on the walls, no brightly colored
wallpaper, no shelves and bric-a-brac. The room is empty
but for the subtle changes of color and texture as the eye
passes from bamboo to pine, from cypress to soft paper
screens, to straw mats on the floors. Even the length and
breadth of the rooms are preordained in multiples of these
standardized floor mats. There is order here and formalism,
and every object that departs from it—a vase, a flower, a
bright silk cushion—has an intensity of visual impact impossible in any other setting.

The focal point of this house and its main room is the
tokonoma, an alcove roughly six feet wide and three feet
deep set in one wall. In times past it was the household
altar, in which the family placed an image of Buddha and
an offering of flowers and incense for daily worship. But
gradually this religious meaning and use of the *tokonoma*
have changed, until today its function is primarily aesthetic,
philosophical, and decorative. There is nothing quite like
it in Western architecture, except perhaps the fireplace and
mantel of our homes. And just as we invite guests to sit before our fireplace for comfort and conversation, so the Japanese seats his guest before the *tokonoma* and entertains him
with the ornamental scroll, flowers, or bonsai arranged
therein.

The traditional Japanese garden is laid out in such a way
that it can always be seen from the *tokonoma.* When we
turn our eyes from the little alcove to the garden, we see
the same forms, ideas, and ideals reflected in every tree,
shrub, and rock. For the purpose of this landscape and bonsai is identical—to capsule the mystery and beauty of nature
for daily contemplation. Bonsai are naturally at home here.

1. In the Japanese home, bonsai are displayed in a special alcove called the *tokonoma*.

2. Where there is no room for a regular garden, bonsai are sometimes used to make a miniature one.

3. Bonsai are usually placed on shelves or benches in an open corner of the garden.

4. Although they are not house plants, bonsai are often brought in for a day.

5. A graceful pine overhanging a garden pool can be wonderfully exciting.

6. Bonsai are particularly effective in the patio, at entrances, or on low walls.

Sometimes when there is no room for a regular garden, bonsai are used to make a miniature one. In a plot the size of a living room rug a complete landscape is created, with tiny trees, stones, bridges, and ponds. By using larger plants and objects in the foreground and proportionately smaller and smaller ones in the farther parts of this tiny garden, an illusion of great depth and distance is created. Once again the Japanese prove themselves masters of perspective and proportion in miniature.

But aside from such special uses, we find bonsai more often simply displayed on shelves or benches in an open corner of the garden. Here they sit waiting to be trained and tended, waiting to be admired in the *tokonoma* again.

BONSAI IN AMERICAN HOMES AND GARDENS

Without the chaste setting of the Japanese home, without the symbolism of the *tokonoma*, without the Buddhist ideology, it might seem useless to bring bonsai into our homes. Yet so great is the magic of these tiny plants that they transcend time and place and creed. Their beauty is universal. It cannot be lost even in our gadget-strewn, television-haunted homes. Placed on our tables, desks, and shelves these tiny trees can still work their wonders, for there is no decorative style that cannot be enhanced by their natural beauty. But using bonsai in the American home calls for a great deal of good taste and common sense.

Perhaps the most obvious and common error in using bonsai for decoration is to attempt an "Oriental" scene. Here the tiny tree is surrounded by gimcrack mandarins, grotesque hunks of driftwood, and all the other props so dear to the heart of at least one species of flower arranger. The result is, of course, both sickening and futile. For if the bonsai is any good at all, it is in itself a perfect living arrangement. To try to improve on it is like putting a hat on Michelangelo's *Moses*.

Of course, it is impossible to dictate taste, but wherever the bonsai is placed in the home, let it stand alone. Give it perhaps a simple screen or hanging for a background—gold for pines and red-berried plants, silver for deciduous trees, bamboo for flowering bonsai and pomegranate.

On a richly polished coffee table a tiny tree can become the center of conversation. Cascading from a simple mantel a chrysanthemum bonsai can fill an autumn room with light. A miniature pine in a shadow box can create a living picture on a bare wall. Good taste and judgment will suggest a hundred other ways to use bonsai in your home.

In the garden we may display bonsai on shelves and benches or arrange them to form miniature landscapes as in Japan. But our penchant for outdoor living will suggest other uses too. Larger specimens are particularly effective in the patio, at entrances, or cascading from low garden walls. A large, tubbed pine overhanging a garden pool can be wonderfully exciting. An exquisitely trained pink flowering cherry in blue porcelain can bring a spring garden to life. Indeed there are few uses for specimen potted plants that bonsai cannot meet superlatively well. We need only look about our homes and gardens with a little imagination to see a dozen spots that could be made more beautiful with bonsai.

Kinds of Bonsai

CHAPTER IV $\mathcal{T}HERE$ are as many kinds and styles of bonsai as there are trees in nature. They range in size from tiny plants scarcely an inch high to impressive specimens 4 feet or more in height. As they are meant to reproduce trees in their natural state, bonsai come in myriad shapes, forms, and styles. Fortunately, out of this bewildering variety the Japanese have developed a relatively simple system of classifying bonsai by size and shape.

CLASSIFICATION BY SIZE

Bonsai come in four sizes—large, medium, small, and miniature. Large bonsai range in height from 26 to 40 inches or more and are grown in sizable pots or tubs. Some might dispute calling such large plants bonsai at all, but they too have been proportionately dwarfed and trained in the best bonsai traditions and their usefulness in decorating patios, porches, and gardens is indisputable.

A handsome Japanese white or five-needled pine *(Pinus parviflora pentaphylla)*, 50 years old, with gnarled and fissured trunk.

A miniature forest of Yezo spruce. Note the training wires on the two small trees in the foreground left.

The graceful proportions of the white or five-needled pine are no-where better exemplified than in this specimen with five trunks.

This Japanese flowering cherry, a variety of *Prunus subhirtella*, though difficult to train, makes an exquisite bonsai.

The trident maple *(Acer buergerianum)* is justly admired for its impressive roots, here shown clasping a stone.

The Japanese yew is grown as bonsai for its dark evergreen foliage,
deeply fissured trunk, and scarlet berry-like fruit.

This 180-year-old flowering apricot *(Prunus mume)* grew for 120 years in a garden before it was potted as a bonsai 60 years ago.

The five-needled pine is a popular bonsai plant because of its easy culture and perfect proportions. Here it is grown in the cascade style.

The bonsai most commonly seen are the medium-sized, from 12 to 26 inches in height. Because they are easier to move and are in good proportion to the scrolls and ornaments of the *tokonoma,* they have traditionally been the most popular size in Japan.

For American homes and fanciers, however, small bonsai, ranging from 7 to 12 inches, are actually best. With their smaller containers they are easily moved about and a place for them can be found on any window sill or small table indoors. Indeed the Japanese call these *katate-mochi bonsai,* "bonsai that can be carried in one hand."

The most delightful yet most difficult to grow are the miniature bonsai called *mame-bonsai,* or "baby bonsai." This group includes all specimens under 7 inches in height and reaches its ultimate in the *shito-bonsai,* or "finger-tip bonsai," tiny plants in 1-inch pots that can actually be held on the tip of a finger.

CLASSIFICATION BY STYLE

Whether large or small, all bonsai are further classified by the number of plants growing in each pot.

1. *Kabumono.* A pot containing a single plant is called *kabumono.* From this one plant may spring one (*tankan*), two (*sokan*), three (*sankan*), five (*gokan*), or many trunks (*kabudate*). Four trunks or plants in a pot are superstitiously avoided, because the word *four* in Japanese, *shi,* sounds like another word which means *death.*

2. *Yose-ue.* When two or more plants are grown in a pot they are called *yose-ue,* "trunks planted together." According to their number we may have *nihon-yose* (two trunks planted together), *gohon-yose* (five trunks planted together),

and so on. The trees may be all of one kind or several kinds.

One of the difficulties of the *yose-ue* style is keeping all the trees in the pot equally healthy and attractive for any length of time. It is much easier to grow the multiple-trunked *kabumono,* which gives somewhat the same effect with only one plant to manage.

3. *Ne-tsuranari.* The *ne-tsuranari,* or "connected root," style closely resembles the *yose-ue.* However, the several trunks in the pot are not individual plants, but a row of offshoots from a single crawling root that lies exposed above ground.

A similar effect is created by the *ikada-buki,* or "raft-like," style, in which a young, well-branched tree is planted horizontally in a container. The recumbent trunk is covered with soil and the branches which rise from it resemble in time a grove of individual trees.

4. *Ishi-tsuki.* In the *ishi-tsuki,* or "with a stone," style, one or more trees are planted on top a rough stone, either in a pocket of soil or with the bare roots simply clasping the stone and running down the sides into a container of soil below. The effect is highly realistic, suggesting a tree perched on a mountain crag or overhanging a rocky coast.

Once the number of plants in a pot and the disposition of their roots are determined, bonsai are classified again by shape and style of trunk.

1. *Chokkan.* The "upright trunk" bonsai represents a tall tree standing proudly erect in level country. Less formal in appearance is the *moyo-gi,* or "free upright," style, in which the irregular upright growth is traditionally arranged in three tiers to represent heaven, earth, and man.

2. *Shakan.* A "slanting trunk" bonsai imitates a tree

1. Large bonsai, grown in sizable pots or tubs, are best for outdoor use.

2. Medium, small, and miniature bonsai are better for display indoors.

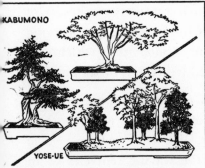

KABUMONO

YOSE-UE

3. A pot containing a single plant is called *kabumono*—more than one plant, *yose-ue*.

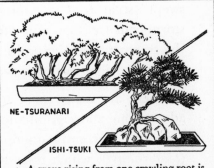

NE-TSURANARI

ISHI-TSUKI

4. A grove rising from one crawling root is called *ne-tsuranari*. Bonsai on a stone, *ishi-tsuki*.

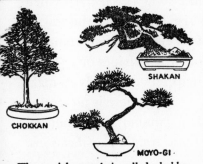

SHAKAN

CHOKKAN

MOYO-GI

5. The upright trunk is called *chokkan*, when irregular *moyo-gi*, when slanting *shakan*.

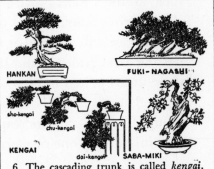

HANKAN

FUKI-NAGASHI

sho-kengai

chu-kengai

KENGAI

dai-kengai

SABA-MIKI

6. The cascading trunk is called *kengai*, the gnarled *hankan*, the windswept *fuki-nagashi*, the decayed *saba-miki*.

growing at right angles to a mountain slope. Its foliage is generally thicker on the side facing the sun. Sometimes this style is called *han-kengai,* or "semi-cascade."

3. *Kengai.* The cascade style, literally called "overhanging a cliff," represents a tree rooted in a high crevice looking down a deep gorge. This style is often likened to a waterfall and classified further as "little fall" (*sho-kengai*), "medium fall" (*chu-kengai*), and "big fall" (*dai-kengai*).

4. *Hankan.* The "gnarled and twisted trunk" bonsai suggests a tree growing on a storm-swept crag. Other styles imitating the effect of wind and weather are the "windswept" style (*fuki-nagashi*), which represents a group of storm-bent trees growing atop a mountain range or along the seacoast; and the "split trunk" (*saba-miki*) which suggests an ancient tree with decayed trunk and torn branches.

There are many more styles of bonsai. Some are free adaptations and combinations of one form with another. Some are currently unpopular, like the "octopus" style (*tako-zukuri*), which resembles the waving tentacles of an octopus, a mode of bonsai still much appreciated in China. Others are simply refinements on the established forms, such as the "roots-above-ground" style (*ne-agari*), which characterizes bonsai whose roots rise high above the soil.

But if we only remember the four sizes, the four common potting arrangements, and the four basic shapes or styles of these dwarf potted trees, it will help immeasurably in making and appreciating bonsai. For actually there is no tree or group of trees, no landscape that cannot be reproduced in miniature by one or more of these simple classifications.

Plants for Bonsai

CHAPTER V $\mathcal{A}LMOST$ any plant can be
grown as bonsai—trees, flowers,
fruit, or grasses. The choice is only limited by our imagination and resourcefulness. But of the countless kinds that
might be grown, there are some that are better suited to
bonsai than others. The deciding factor is proportion. For
a good bonsai must always be in scale, each part perfectly
balanced with the others, to create that magical illusion of
a great tree in miniature.

Some plants are naturally small and well proportioned.
These are easily trained as bonsai. Others have very large
growth, leaves, flowers, or fruit which even the dwarfing
process cannot reduce sufficiently to make them well proportioned. These plants are difficult to train. They seldom
achieve that perfect balance in leaf, blossom, trunk, and
twig that is the secret of the tiny trees.

In selecting plants for bonsai it is important first to know
those kinds that have withstood the test of time and pro-

portion, and then to experiment with new varieties and forms for oneself. The list that follows is by no means exhaustive, but it may give some indication of the wealth of material at our disposal.

EVERGREEN TREES

The coniferous evergreens are probably the most popular of all trees for bonsai. Not only are they naturally abundant in Japan, but they seem to be one of the most unforgettable features of the Japanese landscape. The great avenues of cryptomeria at Nikko and Hakone and the pine-clad islands of the Inland Sea have inspired imitation for centuries. Indeed the conifers are wonderfully adapted by nature to growing as bonsai. Often stunted by weather and privation, rooted in poor rocky soil, they ask only a modicum of care. Yet their sturdy branches and neat evergreen foliage are a source of beauty and inspiration throughout the year.

CEDAR. The deodar, *Cedrus deodara,* is sometimes used for making large bonsai. It is difficult to keep in bounds, however, and not as attractive as *Cedrus atlantica* var. *glauca,* especially the form *compacta.*

CRYPTOMERIA. *Cryptomeria japonica,* the Japanese cedar, or *sugi,* makes splendid bonsai, not only for its majestic form, but because the bright young foliage turns bronze-red or purple in autumn and winter.

CYPRESS. The reddish-brown bark, handsome shape, and shining fan-like branchlets of the Hinoki cypress, *Chamaecyparis obtusa,* makes one of the most popular and easy evergreens for bonsai. The Sawara cypress, *C. pisifera,* is also much used, especially the varieties *filifera, squarrosa,* and *plumosa.*

JUNIPER. Junipers are very easy to train as bonsai and are recommended to the beginner. The most popular is the *shimpaku, Juniperus chinensis,* particularly the prostrate variety *sargenti. J. rigida,* the Mt. Hakone juniper, or *nezu,* is also highly prized for its beautiful form and needle-like leaves.

PINE. Pines occupy the first rank in trees for bonsai because of their beautiful form, long life, and simple culture. The Japanese red pine, or *aka-matsu, P. densiflora,* with its irregular head, orange branchlets, and reddish-brown trunk is quite popular. But the five-needled pine, or *goyo-matsu, P. parviflora,* is the favorite for bonsai because of its easier culture and perfect proportions. Its slender branches with short, blue-green needles are always in scale with the miniature trunk. Much more difficult to shape is the dwarf Siberian pine, or *hai-matsu, P. pumila,* a very dwarf alpine species; and the Korean pine, or *oba-goyo-matsu, P. koraiensis,* which has rather long needles. The needles of the Japanese black pine, or *kuro-matsu, P. thunbergi,* are also too long to be in scale with its handsome trunk and branches. Nevertheless it is a popular plant for bonsai, especially in its thick-barked form called *nishiki-matsu.*

SPRUCE. The Yezo spruce, or *ezo-matsu, Picea jezoensis,* is an ideal plant for bonsai. Its short, dark green needles growing in clusters on every twig are in perfect proportion to the trunk and branches; and the plant is very easy to grow and train, even for beginners.

Yew. The Japanese yew, *onko, Taxus cuspidata,* is grown as bonsai for its dark evergreen foliage, deeply fissured trunk, and scarlet berry-like fruit.

DECIDUOUS TREES

The city dweller who knows the seasons only by the weather and calendar will find a new dimension of time in the deciduous bonsai. Unlike the timeless evergreens, these tiny trees hold a mirror to the changing world around us, reflecting each passing day and hour. In spring they give us hope with bursting buds and blossoms, in summer contentment in rich leaves and fruit, in autumn a bright moment of fulfillment, and in winter the pure cold beauty of sleep. Is it any wonder the Japanese consider the deciduous trees the most poetic, the most elegant of all? Is it any wonder that they have sought to capture the seasons in these tiny, ever-changing boughs?

Beech. The Japanese beech, or *buna, Fagus japonica,* is a tough, handsome tree with silver-gray trunk, delicate leaves in spring, and conspicuous buds in winter. Unlike most deciduous trees, it holds its dead leaves on its twigs until late spring when the new growth appears. This strange habit pleases the Japanese, for by looking at this tree they are reminded of autumn throughout the winter and spring.

Birch. The slender white trunk and handsome form of the Japanese birch, *Betula japonica,* is attractive summer and winter. Several young plants grouped in a shallow container will form an enchanting grove with very little effort.

Carpinus. The red-leafed hornbeam, or *aka-shide, Carpi-*

nus laxiflora, is grown for the bright autumn color of its foliage and its attractive clusters of light-green fruit.

ELM. Japanese elm, or *nire* bonsai, *Ulmus japonica,* are at once graceful and majestic. With their straight trunks, widespreading densely branched heads, they give the illusion of giant forest trees, especially in winter.

GINKGO. The maiden-hair tree, or *icho, Ginkgo biloba,* is highly prized when its fan-shaped leaves turn bright yellow in autumn and the cream-colored fruit develops on female trees.

IVY. The common Japanese or Boston ivy, *Parthenocissus tricuspidata,* although a vine can be kept shrubby by persistent pruning. Old, gnarled stumps are potted and pruned to form quite interesting bonsai that are wonderfully colored in fall.

LARCH. This deciduous conifer, the Japanese larch, or *kara-matsu, Larix leptolepis,* is grown for its rather broad, soft, blue-green needles and handsome red bark.

LIQUIDAMBAR. For its bright autumn color and maple-like leaves the sweet gum, *Liquidambar styraciflua,* is becoming increasingly popular for bonsai. The deeply furrowed trunk and corky branches are very conspicuous in winter.

MAPLE. The most popular of all fall-coloring deciduous trees is the Japanese maple, or *momiji, Acer palmatum.* There are many varieties available ranging in color from deep purple and red through every shade of green, each widely different in size and cut of leaves. Those selected for bonsai should have small, deeply cut leaves that are brightly colored spring and fall.

The trident maple, or *tokaede, Acer buergerianum,* is also very popular for bonsai. It makes a dense growth with neat, fall-coloring leaves and has a tendency to form impressive roots on the surface of the soil.

WILLOW. The weeping willow, or *shidare-yanagi, Salix babylonica,* is prized as a bonsai for its cascading branches and bright spring foliage. It is generally placed on a high stand so that its drooping branches, often 6 feet or more in length, can be seen to advantage.

ZELKOVA. One of the trees especially cultivated for its bare winter beauty is the gray-barked elm, or *keyaki, Zelkova serrata.* It makes a broad, round-topped head with dense branches, small elm-like leaves and handsome trunk.

FLOWERING PLANTS

While we may be impressed by the rugged evergreens, fascinated by the changeable deciduous trees, only flowering plants can give true color and fragrance to bonsai. But finding the right flower is difficult. The rule of proportion will eliminate large blossoms; good taste will eliminate bright colors and strong scents. The flowers must enhance the tiny trees, not detract from them. A giant magnolia bonsai in bloom would be a monstrosity. A gardenia bonsai might distract us by its overpowering fragrance. For these reasons flowering plants for bonsai are usually selected from the wild species, from the small-flowered, delicately colored varieties that can blend quietly into the miniature world of bonsai.

APRICOT. Despite a very common misconception the re-knowned Japanese *ume, Prunus mume,* is not a flowering plum but an apricot. It is perhaps the most-loved flowering plant in Japan, blooming in every home at the New Year season as a symbol of spring. *Ume* bonsai are highly prized for their early bloom, delicate colors and fragrance, and grotesque form. Of the 200 kinds available, preference is given to those with the simplest white blossoms and the oldest, most weathered trunks.

AZALEA. The *tsutsuji,* or azalea, is one of the easiest and most colorful of the flowering bonsai. Plants with small foliage and flowers are generally selected from Satsuki or Kurume varieties.

CAMELLIA. Because of its large flowers and foliage the pop-ular *tsubaki,* or *Camellia japonica,* is unsuited for bonsai. But among the other species, notably *C. sasanqua,* there is a wide variety of neat, small-flowered plants quite perfect for dwarfing.

CHERRY. Despite its popularity, the Japanese cherry, or *sakura,* is one of the most difficult plants to grow as bonsai. The shrubby species such as the *fuji-sakura, Prunus incisa,* and the *takane-sakura, P. nipponica* var. *kurilensis,* are favored for their simple blooms. But the showy garden varieties are effective too if neat, slow-growing, relatively small-flowered kinds are selected.

CHRYSANTHEMUM. Unlike trees and woody plants that take years to develop into good bonsai, chrysanthemums, or *kiku,* are trained and flowered in less than one year. Small, single or anemone, cascade varieties are generally used and trained either in the *kengai* or *ishi-tsuki* style. There is no quicker, less expensive, more floriferous plant for bonsai than the chrysanthemum.

CRAPE MYRTLE. The common crape myrtle, or *saru-suberi, Lagerstroemia indica,* is grown as bonsai for its profusion of blooms in pink, red, purple or white, and for its elegant form and handsome smooth bark.

HAWTHORN. The hawthorn, or *sanzashi, Crataegus cuneata,* provides not only attractive red flowers and fruit, but beautiful small foliage that colors brilliantly in fall.

JASMINE. The *obai,* or *Jasminum nudiflorum,* with its solitary, fragrant, yellow flowers in early spring reminds one of the forsythia. It is prized also for its attractive, twiggy growth. A relative of our star jasmine, *Trachelospermum jasminoides,* the *teika-kazura, T. divaricatum,* a slender, climbing shrub, with buff or pale-orange flowers, is also used for bonsai.

JUNEBERRY. Like the American dogwood, the Japanese juneberry, or *saifuri-boku, Amelanchier asiatica,* blooms in early spring with such a profusion of tiny white flowers that the plant seems covered with snow. Attractive blue fruit follow the flowers.

PEACH AND PEAR. Flowering peach and pear are rarely seen as bonsai, probably because of their relatively large flowers and growth. There are, however, dwarf varieties of both that might make fine specimens.

QUINCE. The dwarf Maule's quince, or *boke, Chaenomeles japonica* not *C. lagenaria,* makes a very ornamental

bonsai with its spreading, spiny branches. The pro-
fuse scarlet flowers appear in early spring before the
glossy foliage and yellow fruit. There are several
varieties with flowers ranging from white to deep
red.

RHODODENDRON. Modern hybrid rhododendrons are, of
course, unsuited for bonsai. But the smaller rock-
garden species such as *R. keleticum, prostratum,*
and *radicans* might make interesting specimens.

ROSE. Though the purist might question their use at all,
roses are sometimes grown as bonsai. Varieties of the
fairy or pygmy rose, *Rosa chinensis* var. *minima,* and
the French rose, *R. gallica* var. *pumila,* might be
used. Even floribunda and multiflora roses have
been dwarfed with some success.

WISTERIA. The Japanese wisteria, or *fuji, Wisteria floribunda,* grows and blooms quite well as bonsai with
flower clusters often 2 feet long. The following kinds
are favored: the wild species, or *yama-fuji,* the rela-
atively dwarf varieties Ebicha and Issai, and the
truly dwarf *W. floribunda* var. *microphylla,* or *hime-
fuji.* The closely related climber *Milletia japonica,*
or *natsu-fuji,* with purple, pink, or white flowers is
also used.

FRUIT AND BERRIES

In Japan, persimmon trees loaded with fruit are such a
common sight in fall that the season is often called "Persimmon Autumn." And indeed it is pleasant to see fruit hanging on trees like so many bits of amber and coral after the
blazing leaves have fallen. The purpose of fruit-bearing
bonsai is to bring the sight of such golden harvests near at

hand. But what was said of flowering trees must be said again of these plants—varieties with large fruit are not suitable for dwarfing. For how can the illusion of a tiny orchard be conjured up by a persimmon, apple, or pear bonsai bearing fruit as big as the pot it is growing in? It is far better to choose the tiny wild fruits and berries for our trees, so that the vital magical proportion of bonsai is never lost.

CELASTRUS. *Celastrus orbiculatus,* or *tsuru-ume-modoki,* is a relative of the American false-bittersweet. It is grown chiefly for its round, orange-yellow fruit with crimson seeds, which become very conspicuous after the leaves have fallen.

CHERRY. *Prunus tomentosa, yusura-ume,* a small, spreading shrub with early white or tinted flowers, is grown chiefly for its bright red, edible fruit.

CITRUS. The round kumquat, or *kinkan, Fortunella japonica,* a much-branched shrub with short spines, is very suitable for bonsai because of its dwarf habit and small, bright orange fruit.

CRAB APPLE. Since ordinary varieties of apple are too large for bonsai, the crab apples are used extensively. One of the finest is the variety Kaido, *Malus micromalus,* which has brilliant red flowers and holds quantities of fruit throughout the winter. Other popular kinds are *M. baccata, prunifolia, sieboldi,* and *halliana.*

EUONYMUS. Many varieties of the spindle tree, or euonymus, are grown in Japan for their variegated leaves and variously colored fruit. But the deciduous *mayumi,* or *E. europaeus,* is the most popular for bonsai with its showy pinkish-red fruit in fall.

HOLLY. The *ume-modoki,* or *Ilex serrata,* with its finely serrated leaves, small pink flowers, and long-lasting vermilion berries makes a most popular winter bonsai.

PERSIMMON. While ordinary persimmons can be dwarfed and made to bear extraordinary fruit, the tiny date plum, or *mame-gaki, Diospyros lotus,* is preferred as being more in scale. In autumn its glossy foliage turns red and the tiny, half-inch fruit slowly ripen from yellow to deep purple.

PHOTINIA. The *kamatsuka,* or *Photinia villosa,* has attractive white flowers, colorful deciduous leaves in fall, and bright red berries through the winter.

POMEGRANATE. After spring flowers fade, the pomegranate, or *zakuro, Punica granatum,* bears its showy blooms in midsummer, followed by a profusion of small red fruit into winter. The dwarf variety *nana* makes excellent bonsai.

PYRACANTHA. The firethorns, or *tokiwa-sanzashi, Pyracantha coccinea* and *angustifolia,* are popular bonsai plants because of their bright red or orange winter berries. They are a good plant for the novice to experiment with, especially some of the fine new hybrids.

GRASSES, HERBS, AND ORNAMENTALS

If the flowering bonsai belong to spring and the deciduous to autumn and winter, the grasses and herbs are certainly the summer bonsai. But although they are popular with amateurs, the connoisseur too often considers them scarcely worth growing at all. Compared with the mighty pines and scarlet maples these wildlings are poor things indeed—transient, homely, without market value. But even in them the entombed city dweller can see for a while the fields and meadows, can feel the seasons change, can live once more as man was meant to live.

BAMBOO. The bamboo, or *take,* is the most important and difficult of the grasses used for bonsai. Dwarf varieties such as *Sasa pumila, humilis,* and *pygmaea;* delicate-leafed kinds such as the *Bambusa multiplex* varieties Chinese Goddess and Striped-stem Fern Leaf; and the popular golden bamboo, *Phyllostachys aurea,* are all possibilities.

FERNS. Dwarf ferns and selaginella—especially the resurrection plant, or *iwahiba, Selaginella lepidophylla,* and *katahiba, S. caulescens*—are sometimes grown as bonsai.

GRASSES. The eulalia, or *susuki, Miscanthus sinensis;* the Japanese sweet-flag, or *sekisho, Acorus gramineus,* and several other grassy plants are used for bonsai.

PALMS. Few of the true palms have been dwarfed successfully except perhaps the windmill palm, *Trachycarpus fortunei* var. *surculosus* and the *Rhapis excelsa* and *humilis.* But the so-called sago palm, or *sotetsu, Cycas revoluta,* has long been a favorite bonsai plant.

PERENNIALS. There is a wide range of dwarf herbaceous perennials and alpines that might be used for bonsai, either alone or with other plants. Two good examples are *Thalictrum kiusianum* and *Erodium chamaedryoides.*

REEDS. The common reed, or *ashi, Phragmites communis;* the Japanese reed, *P. macer;* and the giant reed, *Arundo donax,* all have been dwarfed for bonsai.

RUSHES AND SEDGES. The common scouring-rush, *Equisetum hyemale,* and the umbrella plant, *Cyperus alter-*

nifolius var. *gracilis,* make very elegant dwarf potted plants for indoor decoration.

WATER PLANTS. Several species of water plants including the East Indian lotus, *Nelumbo nucifera,* have been successfully dwarfed.

A visit to any nursery will reveal a hundred other plants as suitable for bonsai. What autumn tree can surpass the gorgeous year-round color of *Nandina domestica?* What berried plant can match the show of *Ochna multiflora* and the tiny cotoneasters? What weeping willow can match the evergreen grace of *Pittosporum phillyraeoides?* The list is endless.

Even in our fields and meadows plants for bonsai abound. Californians have used their native oaks, sequoia, and manzanita with outstanding success. Southerners have contributed the bald cypress and sour gum of their swamps. Enthusiasts in the East and North have found a score of woodland plants and conifers that might make splendid dwarfed trees. The materials for bonsai are all around us, even in our own gardens. But we won't see them unless we are looking for bonsai; we won't recognize them unless we are under the spell of the tiny trees.

Collecting, Buying, and Propagating

CHAPTER VI $\mathcal{P}LANTS$ for bonsai have been collected from the fields and mountains of Japan for centuries—naturally dwarfed trees and shrubs, gnarled and twisted by wind and weather, stunted by privation. In high mountain gorges, on steep island cliffs, in dank bogs and dry rocky slopes, these hard-bitten trees have struggled for ages, until with time they have become nature's own bonsai, more wonderfully shaped and dwarfed than the hand of man could ever hope to fashion. It is these chance natural specimens that the collectors have sought and treasured, braving danger and disappointment with rare skill and courage.

The story of one such collector is charmingly told by Kan Yashiroda, in the Brooklyn Botanic Garden's journal, *Plants and Gardens* (New Series, Vol. 6, No. 2):

A professional collector once told me a story of the toil and superstition of his collecting, which will well illustrate how such collecting is done for a livelihood. By his keen eyes or with the aid of a field-glass, from far beneath on the cliff, he first finds a nice tree—which often may vanish into the fog above. He then seeks a suitable spot near the edge of the cliff where he may sleep for the night. Next, he draws a circle some six feet in diameter and stands on the edge of it. He takes off his upper cloth, or working coat, and places it within the circle, facing toward him. The coat is a substitute for his Deity, and he places grains of rice before it as an offering. Then he prays solemnly, "I am a dwarf tree collector by profession. Please let me rent the spot for the night." After the prayer is done, feeling that he will not encounter or meet with mischief from long-nosed goblins or monsters, he rests for the night.

In the morning he ties firmly one end of a rope to a tree trunk on the cliff's edge and the other end to his body. Holding the coiled ropes and tools such as hammer and chisel, which are used to remove the roots from the rock, and with saw, scissors and knife, he gradually works his way downward to the tree, moving along the cliff. Often the tree is growing on the concave part of the cliff, perhaps underneath a protruding rock; in such cases he lowers himself by the rope to the nearby desired dwarf tree, and then swinging himself, he patiently awaits a chance to grasp the tree or the cliff nearby where he can reach the tree. The digging is a most patient and laborious work, taking many hours. Roughly describing his routine of work, the old-timer had frightened me, telling with an exaggerated gesture, how, had he not prayed, the goblin or monster might come and untie the rope while he worked on the cliff below.

Actually there are many more difficulties encountered in collecting bonsai than warding off goblins and monsters. Sometimes the tiny trees cannot be taken by simply breaking and chiselling the rock around their roots. In the high mountains at the farthest edge of the timberline where the trees are stunted by thin soil and almost impossible climatic conditions, the collector must often root-prune a tree for several successive years before he dares to lift it. Each year he digs on one side of the plant, trimming the far-ranging roots close to the trunk and then filling back with good soil, until after two or three years the plant has developed a compact new root system and can be moved safely.

Even in more favorable locations the Japanese show extraordinary skill in transplanting trees of almost any size and age. The work is usually done in spring just as the sap is rising. A trench is carefully dug around the tree, cutting all the roots except the tap-root and leaving a ball of soil around the plant approximately a foot in diameter and about half as deep. Then straw rope, matting, or burlap is firmly wound in several layers over the sides, top and bottom of the ball to hold the soil about the roots. Finally the tap-root is sawed through and the tree removed. When one considers the trunk of the tree may be three or more inches in diameter this tiny root ball may seem perilously small, but the plants are so skillfully handled that more than 70 per cent survive to become good bonsai.

The newly dug trees are quickly taken to a nursery where all unnecessary branches and damaged roots are carefully pruned. Then with as much original soil as possible still adhering to the roots, they are planted in a bed of sand or sandy loam in the ground, in a wooden box, or unglazed training pot. A shade is put over the plants through the summer to protect them from sun and wind, and they are sprayed frequently with water to moisten the leaves and branches. After two or three years the plant will develop a compact new root system and regain its strength. Then it is planted in an appropriate bonsai pot, tended and established again for another year before training and shaping begin.

These naturally stunted trees make the finest, most highly prized bonsai because they are at once so wonderfully old and realistically shaped. It is no wonder that collectors have virtually exhausted the supply in Japan. Where one could once find fine old plants of Sargent's juniper in Iyo and Echigo provinces, Japanese black pine in Shodoshima, and Yezo spruce in Hokkaido and the Kurile Islands, there is now scarcely anything worth taking. Even Korea has been scoured for Korean mountain cherry, boxwood, and Japanese yew. The old orchards of Japan have been picked clean of fine old stumps of flowering apricot, cherry, and wisteria. That one-plant-in-a-thousand that nature has perfectly fashioned for bonsai is rapidly becoming extinct, and more and more the nursery-grown plant has taken its place.

BUYING PLANTS

Since most bonsai are grown today from small trees and shrubs started in nurseries, it is important to know how and what to buy. Shopping for bonsai material is quite different than choosing plants for ordinary use. The stiffly staked, upright specimens, perfectly symmetrical and full, that we buy for landscaping are practically worthless for bonsai. What we want now are interestingly misshapen plants, three to ten years old, irregularly branched, with low horizontal growths. The trunk and branches should be thick and stocky and the plant broadly pyramidal in shape, with a compact root system showing a few stout roots near the surface. This does not mean, however, that we are looking for overgrown, junky stock; for badly neglected, root-bound material is difficult to reestablish and practically useless. What we do want are healthy plants that have been steadily root-pruned and transplanted, but have somehow developed an interestingly irregular shape that might be further developed as bonsai.

The nurseryman, who usually tries to grow his plants as uniformly as he can, is only too glad to get rid of these odd specimens. Indeed, they occur so rarely in his stock that the bonsai enthusiast will do well to find one really exciting plant in a thousand. But the hunt for material is half the fun of making bonsai. Each plant we find will suggest its own form—one will naturally become a cascade, another a proud upright tree, another a quiet grove. After a while we'll be able to recognize that one plant, the perfect plant, every time. For the real problem in buying plants for bonsai is not cost, but finding the right size, shape, and quality. That is why so many enthusiasts eventually turn to growing their own stock.

SEEDS

If one has patience, excellent bonsai may be grown from seed. The popular beeches, birch, cryptomeria, ginkgo, holly, maple, pines, pomegranate, spruce, and zelkova are all easily grown this way—and less popular plants, too, like the Japanese chestnut, or *kuri;* the parasol tree, or *aogiri;* the wax tree and lacquer tree, *Rhus succedanea* and *verniciflua.* The list is long, as long as the years it takes to make a finished plant of any of these from seed.

Each variety will require slightly different handling from the start. Some seeds are ready for sowing as soon as they are ripe. Others need two to three months of after-ripening, stratified in sand or moss and kept either warm or refriger-

HOW TO CHOOSE PLANTS FOR BONSAI

1. Collecting natural bonsai from fields and mountains is difficult and dangerous work.

2. Nursery-grown plants are the easiest and best source for bonsai. Seeds and cuttings require time and patience.

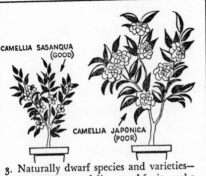

CAMELLIA SASANQUA
(GOOD)

CAMELLIA JAPONICA
(POOR)

3. Naturally dwarf species and varieties—with small flowers, foliage, and fruit—make the best bonsai.

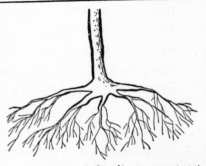

4. A good bonsai plant has a compact root system with heavy surface roots on all sides.

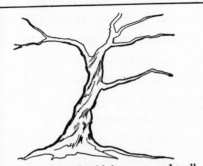

5. The trunk should be stout and well shaped to make training easier and create the illusion of great age.

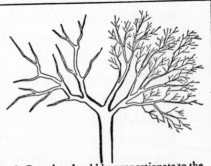

6. Branches should be proportionate to the trunk, full on all sides, and well developed to the tips.

ated. Seeds with very hard coats must be notched, cracked, or softened by soaking in hot water or acid. Some seeds will germinate in one month; others, in two years. Only experience and observation can determine what each seed will require. But when it comes to planting, they are all treated pretty much alike.

Seeds for bonsai are usually sown soon after ripening in standard nursery flats or seed pans that are about 3 inches deep. To provide good drainage a ½-inch layer of fine gravel or potshards is spread over the bottom, then the flat is filled with 2 inches of sandy loam or a mixture of equal parts coarse sand, leaf mold or dampened peat moss, and soil. The seed bed is smoothed and pressed lightly. Then the seeds are placed an inch or two apart over the surface and covered to their own thickness with sand or the soil mixture sifted and pressed down over them. The flat is then placed in a warm, half-shaded location under a tree, in a lath house, or frame and carefully watered with a fine spray until the soil is saturated. A pane of glass or square of burlap is placed over the seed pan to prevent excessive evaporation and help the seed germinate more quickly.

As soon as the seedlings appear the glass or burlap should be removed and the flat kept moderately damp. When the little plants have produced two or three leaves, they should be transplanted to individual 2- or 3-inch pots containing much the same kind of soil mixture as that in which they germinated. If the seedlings have made a strong tap-root it should be cut back by one third to encourage more root branching, and the slender side roots carefully spread in the pot so that they will develop evenly near the surface. Training to any preconceived shape may be begun even at this stage. The seedlings may be planted on a slant in the pots, the tips of young shoots may be pinched to force lateral branches, or the young plants may be tied to a bamboo cane to insure a straight trunk. In short, in a few years we can make our seedling that ideal bonsai plant that is so hard to find and almost impossible to buy in nurseries. The only thing we need is time.

CUTTINGS

For those who are impatient, bonsai grown from cuttings will give much quicker results. The countless plants that can be grown in this way are divided into three basic groups. First are the Softwood Cuttings, like the chrysanthemum, taken in spring or early summer from the soft new growth and easily rooted in three or four weeks. Next are the Semi-hardwood Cuttings—like the azaleas, conifers, cotoneaster, jasmine, and pyracantha—made in midsummer and fall of the nearly ripened new growth. Last are the Hardwood Cuttings—like the crape myrtle, pomegranate, quince, willow, and wisteria—made in fall and winter from ripe wood of the past season.

The first two groups are handled in much the same way. Cuttings are taken from non-flowering, vigorous tip shoots of healthy plants. They are usually from 2 to 4 inches in length and the base is trimmed with a sharp knife $\frac{1}{4}$ inch below a node or growth bud. All leaves on the lower half of the cutting are removed, but as many as possible are kept on the top half to provide food until the new roots have formed. The use of rooting hormones is optional.

Standard nursery flats filled three inches deep with damp builder's sand or a mixture of half sand and half dampened peat moss are ideal for rooting the cuttings. The medium should be leveled and tamped firmly with a board or brick.

Then using a stout knife a narrow trench is cut the length and depth of the flat and the prepared cuttings are inserted, leaving their leaves above the surface and far enough apart so they do not crowd or touch each other. When one row is filled, a narrow board or brick is placed alongside it and tamped heavily until the cuttings and sand are firmed. Each row or flat is labeled as to variety, date, and number of cuttings set, and then placed in a lightly shaded spot under a tree, in a lath house, or frame. Once set in place the cuttings should be soaked thoroughly, but thereafter watered only enough to prevent wilting. When the cuttings have made about an inch of root growth they are taken up and potted like seedlings.

The third group or Hardwood Cuttings are handled a bit differently. They are made from ripened wood 6 to 8 inches long, about the thickness of a lead pencil, with at least two growth eyes or nodes to each cutting. Tip growth is discarded in favor of the thicker lower sections. These dormant cuttings, tied in bundles, are packed in boxes filled with damp soil, sand, peat, or sawdust to callus over winter in a cool place. In spring they are lifted and rooted in flats or pots like any other cutting. Hardwood cuttings are valuable for bonsai because they produce a stout-trunked plant almost immediately. Cuttings up to an inch in diameter can be rooted of such plants as willow, ivy, ginkgo, and holly.

Not all plants will grow satisfactorily from cuttings, however. Most fruit and nut trees, maple, oak, birch, linden, and beech must either be grown from seeds or grafted and budded.

GRAFTING AND LAYERING

Unfortunately grafting, the quickest propagating method of all, is seldom used for bonsai. The chief objection to it up till now has been that the union or joint between root-stock and scion is usually too visible and badly scarred, thus spoiling the appearance of the plant. But with improved grafting methods this handicap may be removed entirely, for modern propagators can join two plants so skillfully that it is almost impossible to tell where the union is made.

Grafting is the process of bringing together the growing regions of two related plants to make them unite and grow as one. The growing tissues of plants are contained in a very thin layer of cells between the bark and wood, the cambium layer, which produces new wood and bark cells for the plant. Successful grafting is simply matching the cambium layers of understock and scion as closely as possible. Actually a scion is a cutting which, instead of being placed in sand to form its own roots, is inserted into the root system of another plant. Thus, selecting good scion wood is the same as selecting good cutting wood. The best time for grafting is in spring, about 60 days before new growth starts.

There are three methods of grafting that are particularly suitable for bonsai because they seldom leave noticeable scars at the union. The Whip or Tongue Graft uses stock and scion of the same diameter. Both are cut on a long slant; a slit is made in the middle of each cut surface and the two are fitted together so that the tongue of one fits into the slot of the other. They are then bound firmly with raffia and the union covered with grafting compound. The Whip Graft may either be made on a trunk or branch or directly on a piece of root, in which case it is called a Root Graft. Another method, especially useful for developing branches at bare spaces along the trunk or main limbs of bonsai, is the Side Graft. In this method a long cut is made downward into the stock just beneath the bark, and the scion (its base cut wedge-shaped) is snugly fitted into the cut, tied there and sealed. The very neat Veneer Graft is similar to the Side Graft except that the stock, instead of simply having a wedge cut into it has a wedge cut out of it, and the scion is trimmed to fit the resulting notch exactly. With any method of grafting, however, it is absolutely necessary to have the cambium layers of stock and scion aligned and touching on at least one side of the graft to insure success.

The advantages of grafting bonsai are, of course, apparent. Branches of fine varieties can be grafted onto old, gnarled roots, creating superb specimens overnight. Poorly shaped plants can be transformed by grafting new branches wherever they are needed. Rare plant forms such as the thick-barked Japanese black pine can be grafted onto the common varieties. A branch can be bent and grafted to its own trunk or to the trunk of another tree. Natural dwarfs may be produced by grafting onto dwarfing understocks. The possibilities are endless, yet they have scarcely been explored.

In sharp contrast, layering as a method of propagating plants for bonsai has been used from antiquity. It is particularly effective because the resulting plants are larger and heavier than can ordinarily be raised from cuttings. The process of rooting large branches while they are still attached to the parent plant is extremely simple. There are three common methods.

The Bowed-branch Layer is made by bending a long

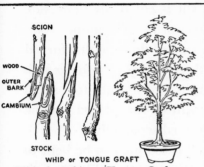

WHIP or TONGUE GRAFT

1. With the Whip or Tongue Graft rare varieties may be grafted onto the trunk, branch, or root of common bonsai plants.

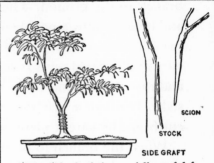

SIDE GRAFT

2. The Side Graft is especially useful for developing branches at bare spaces along the trunk or main limbs.

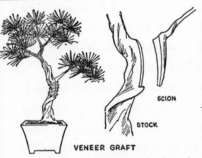

VENEER GRAFT

3. With Veneer Grafting poorly shaped plants can be transformed by grafting new branches wherever they are needed.

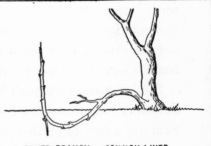

BOWED BRANCH or COMMON LAYER

4. Almost any woody plant capable of being bent to the earth can be rooted by Common Layer.

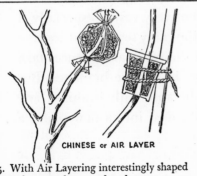

CHINESE or AIR LAYER

5. With Air Layering interestingly shaped branches may be rooted and grown on as husky, "ready-made" bonsai.

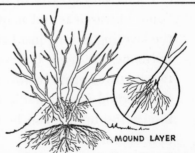

MOUND LAYER

6. Mound and other layers produce larger plants than can be ordinarily raised from cuttings, but the roots are not always as dependable.

branch to the ground. Then a slit is cut in its underside and held open by a pebble or sliver of wood to induce rooting. The cut portion is carefully pegged down with a forked wire and covered with two or three inches of potting soil, and the exposed end of the plant is tied upright to a small stake. In about a year the layer will be rooted and may be cut from the parent plant and potted separately.

When the branch to be layered is too high to be bent to the ground, Chinese or Air Layering is used. The stem is notched as usual where the roots are to form, and the area is covered with a large ball of damp soil, peat, or sphagnum moss. The material is held in place by a special air-layering pot or a tight bandage of burlap, raffia, or plastic. The rooting medium is kept moist until roots form in it, then the branch is cut off below the new roots and potted.

Mound Layers are made by cutting deciduous plants such as quince to within a few inches of the ground in spring and heaping a foot of earth over the stumps. The stumps send up new shoots that root in the mound of earth during the year and these new plants are then removed and potted separately the next spring.

Plants vary greatly in their ability to grow from layers. Some like azaleas and maples root very easily, especially if the layering is done just before the rainy season and rooting hormones are used. Others like the pines and spruces take two or three years to form roots in mature branches. But the method is a valuable one, because with it almost any interesting branch can be transformed into a new plant, a new bonsai.

IMPORTING

To those who cannot wait at all, who must have fine specimen bonsai at any cost, the idea of importing plants from Japan will occur sooner or later. In times past this was a relatively simple matter. Wonderful bonsai could be imported with very little effort or expense. In fact, most of the really fine plants in America today are those that were brought from Japan before the sweeping Plant Quarantine Law No. 37 was laid down in 1919.

Since that time importing bonsai has been a risky business, hedged in by a hundred restrictions. Application for a permit must first be made to the United States Department of Agriculture, Bureau of Entomology and Plant Quarantine, Import and Permit Section, Hoboken, New Jersey. The application must state the quantity and designation of the plants, name and address of the foreign shipper, country and locality in which grown, foreign port of departure, U.S. port of first arrival, U.S. port of entry (if other than port of first arrival), whether importation is to be made by mail, name and address of person to whom permit should be mailed if other than the applicant, and the signature of the applicant, street address, city, and state.

The Department of Agriculture assumes no responsibility for the plants while in its custody, either from lack of specialized care or injury from fumigation. It does suggest that the plants be imported while dormant, because they can only be shipped bare root with moistened peat, sphagnum, sawdust, coconut fiber, excelsior, shavings, buckwheat hulls or cereal chaff (except rice hulls) packed about their roots. Plants shipped in sand or soil may be refused on arrival at the inspection station.

If bonsai are carried as personal baggage the passenger may apply for a permit on arrival, although it is preferable to have this arranged in advance. The plants may clear quarantine only at approved stations such as Honolulu, San Francisco, Seattle, Hoboken, Miami, Laredo, and San Juan, Puerto Rico. If the port of arrival is not an approved inspection station the plant must be shipped at the applicant's expense to the nearest approved station.

In addition to these precautions there is a long list of specific plants that require post-entry quarantine, and a longer list still of plants that cannot be imported at all. Since these regulations change periodically, it is best to write the Department for the latest instructions before ordering plants abroad. Of course, these laws were not made simply to prevent us from importing bonsai, but to protect us from a thousand plant pests and diseases of which we know nothing yet. Actually, the quarantine may be a blessing in disguise, for because of it many more will make bonsai for themselves, many more will find the real secret of bonsai that cannot be bought with money.

This 30-year-old *goyo-matsu* makes a strangely beautiful picture
with its irregular upright growth.

The Japanese maple *(Acer palmatum)* is the most popular of all fall-coloring trees. This 80-year-old specimen shows the delicate beauty of the *momiji* foliage.

Kurume azaleas with small flowers and foliage make wonderful
flowering bonsai.

One of the trees especially cultivated for its bare winter beauty is the zelkova, or gray-barked elm. Note the perfectly developed network of branches and twigs in this fine specimen.

Containers and Soil

C*H O O S I N G* the right containers for bonsai is as important as selecting the right plants. Bonsai are traditionally grown in small ceramic trays, pans, or dishes of many sizes, shapes, and colors. The bonsai fancier spends much time selecting the right container, for it must harmonize perfectly with the plant. Good bonsai pots are elegant and expensive, subdued in color and graceful in form. They are to bonsai what frames are to paintings.

Originally, clay pots from the Iking area in China were considered the most beautiful and desirable for bonsai. But as they were rather rare and expensive, Japanese kilns soon began turning out a flood of imitations. Today the Japanese have a virtual monopoly in this field, producing a splendid variety of containers at relatively low cost. Although a few California potteries have recently ventured to make bonsai pots, the best and cheapest are still those imported from Japan. They are usually sold here by bonsai dealers, nurs-

51

eries, and Oriental import shops, and are priced from about 75¢ to $25 each, depending on quality and size.

Bonsai pots usually come in graduated sets of three containers, each a different size but all the same shape and color. They may be glazed or unglazed—made of plain low-fired terra cotta for cheap training pots to fine glazed ware for show containers. But regardless of quality they are never brightly colored or showy. Since the object of bonsai is to suggest a landscape, the color of the container is felt to be symbolic of earth and rocks. So most bonsai pots are in quiet colors—dark brown, gray, black, dark red, or dark purple. Evergreen conifers, for example, are traditionally given dull white or brown pots; deciduous trees and shrubs, soft gray or blue. Bonsai with red flowers are planted in off-white containers, white flowers in dull red, and yellow flowers in blue. Old pots with a soft patina overlying the color are prized for aged bonsai, but young plants are given new unglazed containers.

It may be well-nigh impossible for us who have endured the same, hideous, red clay pots for generations to understand the subtle relationship the Japanese sees between each plant and its container. For unlike our ugly functional pots, these bonsai dishes do far more than simply hold a plant. They are a vital part of an artistic composition. They are a skillfully chosen frame for a living picture. And just as a fine frame enhances and projects the painting it holds, so the right pot complements and completes the bonsai it contains. It is this perfect harmony, this perfect proportion of tree and pot together, that creates the magical illusion of bonsai. That is why there must be a special color, shape, and size of pot for every kind of plant.

Bonsai pots range in size from 2 to 25 inches in diameter

and from 1 to 10 inches in depth. They are always relatively small and shallow, rarely more than one fourth as large as the trees they contain. But whether round, oval, oblong, square, rectangular, or diamond-shaped, finding the proper proportion in size between tree and pot is an extremely important factor in creating a balanced picture.

All bonsai containers may be divided into two basic types: glazed dishes and basins holding water in which bonsai are simply displayed; and second, regular pots filled with soil in which bonsai are actually grown. In the first kind of container we usually find water plants or clumps of grass and rushes arranged to suggest a pond or lake. Sometimes, too, bonsai growing on stones or mounds of soil are placed in shallow trays of water to form a miniature seascape. But these containers filled with water can be used only for bog plants or when the bonsai is raised on a rock or mound to ensure drainage.

All other bonsai pots must have drainage holes in the bottom to allow excess water to drain off and to permit aeration of the soil. The smaller containers have one hole and the larger ones have three to five each. These drainage holes, sometimes called "eyes," must be partially closed in potting to prevent the soil from washing out. The simplest cover is a bit of broken flower pot placed concave side down over the hole. But the Japanese have also devised little perforated clay covers, or "eyelids," shaped like an inverted teacup which fit over the drainage hole. However these "eyelids" displace too much soil in the tiny pots, so that a flat, ceramic cover honeycombed with holes has recently come into use. Actually the best cover of all is a one-inch square of aluminum window screen simply laid over the drainage hole.

From all this it might seem that the only suitable pots for bonsai are made of clay. But in times past fine Chinese and Japanese bronze trays were very popular too. And there have always been wooden containers, simple and inexpensive, which even the poorest bonsai enthusiast might make for himself. Indeed these rude trays and boxes made of rough weathered wood are often more beautiful and effective than anything one can buy. They can be made in any shape or size, of old redwood, cypress, or driftwood. And because they hold moisture better than clay, they are actually easier to maintain. Certainly there is no excuse for not growing bonsai because one cannot get imported pots. Wonderful collections have been started in sardine cans, cigar boxes, even on a piece of tile picked up in the streets of a bombed-out city.

SOIL FOR BONSAI

Because bonsai pots are so small the kind of soil they contain is extremely important. But there are so many different potting mixtures recommended by the experts that the beginner is usually at a loss to know which one is best. Actually all these elaborate formulas are trying to achieve the same result—to grow the finest plant in the least amount of soil.

The ideal potting soil for bonsai is one which can hold the greatest amount of food and water and at the same time afford perfect drainage and aeration. There are four basic ingredients in that soil:

1. *Clay.* Hard clay subsoil is dried, broken, and screened into uniform granular pellets of various sizes. When used in potting mixtures these rough pellets promote aeration

by forming tiny open pockets or spaces in the soil which alternately fill with water when the soil is saturated, and with air as it dries out. This continuous interchange of air and water allows plant roots to "breathe" and grow freely.

The Japanese use several varieties of clay soil; the most famous is the light-yellow Kanuma clay which is commonly used in potting azaleas. A fair substitute may be made by treating any heavy clay soil with one of the new chemical conditioners to form a granular aggregate. Other materials that give much the same aerating action as clay pellets in the soil are granulated charcoal and perlite.

2. *Loam.* Unlike hard clay subsoils which contain little organic matter or food value, rich loamy topsoils are used primarily to give bonsai much-needed nourishment. Any good garden loam or fibrous turf loam rubbed between the hands to a granular condition is acceptable.

3. *Sand.* Sharp sand and gravel loosen potting soils and increase their porosity and drainage. Indirectly they also improve root development, for when fibrous roots strike the particles of sand in the soil they turn aside or branch and thus form a more extensive network throughout the pot.

4. *Humus.* Peat moss, peat humus, leaf mold, or chopped sphagnum moss are used in bonsai soils to help hold moisture, add slowly decaying humus and plant food, and provide acidity for acid-loving plants. Peat and sphagnum moss should always be thoroughly dampened before being used.

All bonsai potting mixtures are a combination of two or more of these basic ingredients—the exact proportions of which are determined by the natural soil requirements of each kind of plant, its stage of development, and local growing conditions. In Japan professional soil merchants bring the various kinds of clay, sand, soil, and humus from the countryside to the big cities. Bonsai collectors purchase these raw materials, mix them thoroughly in the proper proportions, and pass the resulting mixture through a half-dozen different screens to give soil particles measuring from ⅜ to 1/32 of an inch.

In potting, these variously sized particles of soil are arranged in layers, ranging from the largest at the bottom to the finest at the top. Small or shallow pots usually have three layers of the smaller soil particles. Very large or tall pots may have as many as six different layers to ensure good root growth and quick drainage.

There are as many soil mixtures for bonsai as there are enthusiasts. Each grower has his own pet formulas and secrets, each expert his own "expert" opinions. But, strange to say, these dwarfed plants are more adaptable and easily satisfied than the people who grow them. If the truth be told, all any bonsai requires is a reasonable facsimile of its native soil. Dry mountain plants need lean, gritty soil; plants from peat bogs thrive in moist, acid soil; trees from the fertile valleys want soft, rich loam. Remembering that, one cannot go far wrong in making his own potting mixtures. But it may help to cite here the potting formulas of one Japanese grower. For conifers in development he uses 5 parts clay, 3 loam, 2 sand; after attaining final shape 6 clay, 3 sand, 1 loam. Deciduous trees and broad-leaved evergreens in development get 7 parts loam, 3 clay, 1 leaf mold; after attaining final shape 2 loam, 2 clay, 1 sand. Elms, zelkovas, and maples 7 clay, 3 loam, 1 leaf mold. Bamboos and willows 3 loam, 1 clay, 1 leaf mold. Flowering and fruit trees 8 loam, 2 clay, 1 leaf mold. Rhododendrons and azaleas

7 parts clay (Kanuma clay), 3 chopped sphagnum or peat moss. Chrysanthemums 3 loam, 2 leaf mold, 1 sand.

Although these mixtures have worked well for one grower in one particular locality, it is not certain that they will work as well everywhere else. There is nothing sacred about these formulas. Growers in cool, wet areas may have to alter them to get better drainage; growers in hot, dry areas may add more moisture-holding ingredients. Some may abandon all special formulas and adopt one all-purpose mixture in which to grow any and all bonsai. One British grower has done just that with splendid results using 2 parts fibrous loam, 2 parts coarse silver sand, and 1 part flaky leaf mold. Actually the technique of making bonsai soils is not a matter of formulas or schedules, but one which calls for much common sense and careful observation.

Potting Bonsai

CHAPTER VIII *W* H EN the tree collected in the mountains has developed a new root system, when the seedlings and cuttings we have raised have grown to just the right size, when the "find" we made in the nursery seems very promising—it is time to pot bonsai. Depending on their variety and the locality in which they are grown, bonsai are potted at various times of the year. Conifers, grasses, broad-leaved evergreens, deciduous trees, summer- and fall-flowering plants are usually potted in early spring just before growth buds begin to swell. Spring-flowering plants like the apricot, cherry, and azalea are potted after they finish blooming. Fast-growing plants such as the willow and crape myrtle are potted twice each year, once in spring and once in midsummer. Hardy fruit-bearing trees such as cherry, quince, apple, and pear are usually potted in early autumn. So too are the berried plants like the cotoneaster, hawthorn, juneberry, pyracantha, and photinia. But few if any bonsai are potted in late autumn or winter.

HOW TO POT BONSAI

Whether our plants have just come from the field, the nursery, or are already established bonsai, the technique of potting is essentially the same. The first consideration is selecting an appropriate container. A relatively small pot is, of course, necessary to give the plant little room for root development and to restrain its growth. But although the pot may be shallow it should be of fairly generous width. The average bonsai pot is about one fourth as large as the plant it contains, but with very dwarf or low spreading trees it may be nearly one third as large. Unglazed training pots are best for young plants because they are porous and promote good aeration and root growth. Older plants may be given any one of the containers described in Chapter VII, according to the grower's tastes.

In order to fit the container we have selected, it is usually necessary to prune the roots of our bonsai plant. Unlike other potted plants that are moved up to a larger container when they are transplanted, bonsai are usually root-pruned and moved down to the smallest possible container in keeping with the plant. This process of root-pruning not only keeps the plant dwarfed, but helps it develop a shallow, compact root system that can be fitted into the size and shape of pot best suited to it.

Root-pruning and potting should be done on a bench protected from sun and wind. Bonsai specialists sometimes use a revolving stand or "Lazy Susan" to facilitate quick handling and turning of the plant. But actually the only tools needed are a sharp knife, scissors, a small trowel, and a pointed lead pencil or stick.

The plant is first carefully removed from its pot, can, or

burlap ball and placed on the bench. The soil about the roots should be moderately dry yet soft. With a jabbing motion of a pencil or pointed stick the soil is gently picked away from the roots on the sides and bottom of the root ball, taking care not to break any more roots than is necessary. Young plants can have as much as two thirds of the soil removed in this way; older specimens, not more than one third. If the plants are to be grown in shallow containers more soil should be removed from the bottom of the ball than the sides. When the proper amount of soil has been removed from the plant, the remaining ball will be about one fourth smaller in diameter than the pot we have selected. The uncovered roots are then trimmed with scissors right up to the remaining ball of soil and the plant is ready to be potted. But good judgment must always be used not to remove too much soil or expose too many roots at once, so that the balance between the plant's top growth and root system is not lost entirely. In preparing heavy-rooted specimens taken from the field or from large containers, it is sometimes better to reduce the soil ball and size of pot gradually over a period of several years rather than risk drastic root-pruning all at once.

The container selected, whether new or old, should be washed thoroughly to remove dirt and stains. Then a piece of broken pot or a 1-inch square of aluminum window screen is placed over the drainage hole. Over this a thin layer of coarse sand (for small pots) or fine gravel (in deeper pots) is laid down for drainage. Then the bottom of the pot is filled with coarse particles of soil screened out of the prepared soil mixture.

The potting soil should be mixed and screened in advance as described in Chapter VII and moistened very

HOW TO POT BONSAI

1. The tools and materials for potting bonsai are few and easily acquired.

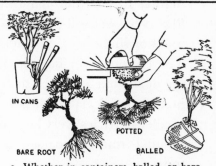

2. Whether in containers, balled, or bare root, bonsai plants must be handled carefully and protected from sun and wind.

3. Good judgment must always be used in reducing the soil ball and pruning the roots.

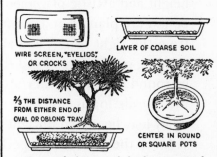

4. Proper drainage, artistic placement, and careful potting insure the health and beauty of bonsai.

LAYERS OF SIFTED SOIL FIRMED WITH STICK

5. Firm potting removes air pockets in the soil and promotes good root action and absorption of water.

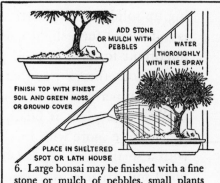

6. Large bonsai may be finished with a fine stone or mulch of pebbles, small plants with moss or ground cover.

slightly to facilitate handling. Very dry soil is difficult to firm; very wet soil packs too tightly. If the pot is relatively small or shallow three grades of soil particles may be used. The bottom layer may be obtained from a 1/4-inch screen, the next from a 1/8-inch screen, and finally soil from a 1/16-inch screen. Very small pots take two or three layers of the smaller particles; very large or tall pots as many as six layers, ranging from the coarsest at the bottom to the finest at the top.

When a layer or two of soil have been laid in the bottom of the container, the bonsai should be tried in the pot for height and artistic placement. In oval or oblong containers bonsai are planted at a point about two thirds the distance from the right or left end and just a trifle to the rear, depending on the spread and shape of the branches. In square or round containers they are planted in the center, except the cascade forms which are planted toward the front edge. They may be potted upright or at an angle.

Once the plant is properly set in the pot, it is pressed down to seat it firmly. Then another layer of soil is added all around and packed firm with a small, blunt stick using a short, jabbing motion. More soil is added as needed, building up solid layers of earth around the plant until the pot is full except for a slight space for watering. It is extremely important to have the soil packed to a uniform hardness throughout the pot, so that air pockets are removed and water can permeate every part evenly.

When the plant is finally set, the surface of the pot is firmed once more with the back of a trowel and smoothed with a small, hard-bristled brush. A very thin layer of the finest soil particles is spooned over the smooth surface and a few pieces of green moss are pressed down into the soil to provide an artistic ground cover. Other delicate ground covers such as baby's tears, *Helxine soleiroli;* Corsican mint, *Mentha requieni;* and *Erodium chamaedryoides* might also be used. A small rock with interesting color or texture may be added to the pot to heighten the naturalistic effect.

The newly planted bonsai is then placed in a lath house, patio, or shelter protected from strong sun and wind and watered thoroughly. A watering can with a very fine spray is passed lightly over the plant again and again until the soil is saturated and drains freely from below. After this initial soaking, the plant may be sprinkled over the leaves and branches frequently, but it will not need much water in the pot until the roots begin to grow again. The plants should be kept under shelter for about two weeks, and then gradually given more and more sun as the roots take hold.

REPOTTING BONSAI

Because bonsai are grown in such small containers they must sooner or later be potted again. The time for repotting varies from twice each year for lusty growers such as the willow and crape myrtle, to once in five to ten years for very dwarf herbaceous plants. Generally all flowering plants, fruit trees, and bamboo are repotted every year. Broad-leaved trees, both evergreen and deciduous, are transplanted once every two years. Coniferous evergreens are repotted once every four or five years.

Unfortunately bonsai do not always keep this schedule. As their roots spread quickly through the tiny pots exhausting every grain of nourishment in the soil, they often need repotting much sooner than expected. Baby bonsai, for example, regardless of variety must be repotted every year. Larger specimens, too, may soon begin to show a decline in vigor, poor color and growth, and become so root-bound that the soil is lifted above the rim of the pot by the crowding roots. Then, regardless of schedules, they must be repotted or die.

The technique of repotting is the same as for potting, except that the plant is root-pruned and returned with new soil to the same container year after year. In this way bonsai are kept dwarf yet healthy in their tiny pots, as new fibrous roots replace old crowded roots and new soil replaces old.

PLANTING BONSAI ON A STONE

Bonsai are not always potted directly in a container. In the *ishi-tsuki*, or "with a stone," style, one or more trees are planted on top of a rough stone, either in a pocket of soil or with the bare roots simply clasping the stone and running down the sides into a container of soil below. The effect is highly artistic, suggesting a rocky tree-clad island or lofty precipice beneath which streams flow or breakers wash. The *ishi-tsuki* bonsai is perhaps the most consciously decorative of all styles, the nearest thing to the formal tray-landscape.

Finding the right stone for this kind of bonsai is often difficult. It must be the right size, shape, and color to harmonize with the plant and container. Yet it must have sizable cavities in its surface in which to plant and crevices along the sides in which roots may grow. If the stone is heavily covered with moss or lichens it will be especially prized, but it must be stable in the container and stand upright. Tufa—a soft, porous volcanic rock that is easily cut and shaped—has all these qualifications and is probably the best kind to use.

Plants for *ishi-tsuki* must also be selected carefully. If they are too big they will have too many bulky roots to fit the stone. If they are too small, the roots will not be long or strong enough. If they are too old or potbound, the roots will be stunted and difficult to train. The ideal *ishi-tsuki* plant is young and vigorous with pliant, active roots that can adapt themselves to this strange way of growing. These strong, young plants actually overtake older specimens, and yet they remain wonderfully dwarfed because most of their roots are developed naturally on the stone.

There are three ways of planting *ishi-tsuki* bonsai. The first and easiest is to find or cut a sizable cavity or pocket in a rock, fill it with rich peaty soil, and plant directly in it. The plant should be quite young, with a compact root system, prepared and pruned for planting in the same way as any other bonsai. The porous rock simply takes the place of an ordinary bonsai pot. But the soil mixture is made somewhat richer and more water-retentive than usual, because water and nourishment drain away from the stone more quickly than from a pot. This type of *ishi-tsuki* planting is usually set in a shallow dish of water, not only to provide moisture for the porous stone and reduce the need for frequent watering, but to suggest a miniature seascape. Occasionally dwarfed perennials such as *Thalictrum kiusianum* or *Acorus gramineus* are also planted on the stone to enhance the effect. These water arrangements make very popular summer bonsai for the home.

The second style of *ishi-tsuki* planting is quite different. A shallow bonsai pot is prepared with drainage and soil just as if it is to receive a plant. But instead, an *ishi-tsuki* stone is placed where the plant would ordinarily stand. Then a young tree with exceptionally long, strong roots is completely bare-rooted, either by gently picking off the soil or, better still, by washing it off in a bucket of water. As long as the work is done quickly in a protected spot the roots will not be harmed. The bare-rooted plant is then carefully set over the stone where it will show to best advantage, and its roots arranged down the sides following the natural crevices in the stone until all the root tips are spread and anchored in the container of soil below. Only dead or very short roots that will not reach the soil in the container are pruned. Then the plant, its root crotch seated firmly on top the stone and its long roots tightly clasping the sides, has its root tips potted as usual in the container. The little plant on "stilts" will need a longer period of shading and after-care to become fully established. But then its roots will quickly grow to embrace the stone and fill the pot below.

The third style of potting *ishi-tsuki* combines features of both the preceding methods. It is used chiefly to make chrysanthemum bonsai. Although the maples, five-needled pine, Chinese juniper, and Yezo spruce are the most commonly used plants for *ishi-tsuki*, chrysanthemums are becoming more and more popular subjects for this style of bonsai. And it is no wonder. In less than nine months, small-flowered single or anemone cascade varieties make finished specimens on stone that would require years to duplicate with other plants.

Softwood chrysanthemum cuttings are made in March and potted singly in 5- or 6-inch pots as soon as they are well rooted. By early May the plants will have several thick, white roots lying near the surface of the soil in the pots. These are the roots that will be made to clasp the surface of the stone and grow down into the container of soil below.

HOW TO PLANT BONSAI ON A STONE

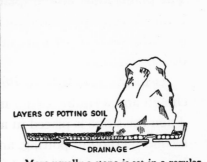

. Bonsai may be planted directly in the avities of a stone and the whole arrangement placed in a tray of water.

2. More usually a stone is set in a regular bonsai pot having drainage and layers of prepared soil.

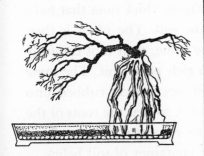

3. The plant is seated atop the stone, its bare roots clasping the sides, and the root tips potted in the container below.

4. Chrysanthemum cuttings are planted atop a stone set in a regular bonsai pot—here made of wood.

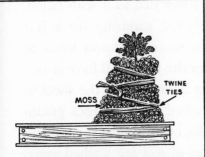

5. The stone is rubbed with pasty soil and covered with sphagnum to induce roots to grow down the sides.

6. By fall the plant fills the container below, the moss is removed, and the bare roots on the stone are revealed.

The plants must be transplanted at just the right moment. If they become potbound there will be too many bulky roots to fit the stone. If they are taken too soon the roots will not be long enough.

As in the first style of *ishi-tsuki,* an interesting stone is chosen and a sizable cavity is cut in it to receive the plant. Then the stone is placed in a bonsai pot as described in the second method of potting, and the container is filled to the brim with the usual layers of potting soil. The young chrysanthemum plant is removed from its pot and the soil carefully picked away from its roots. Most of the exposed roots are cut off, leaving only a few, strong, thick ones that have developed near the surface of the soil. The plant is then placed in the hollow spot on the stone, each root carefully spread, and planted firmly with rich peaty soil. The same soil dampened to a pasty consistency is next rubbed into dents and crevices all over the stone, so that the roots of the plant will find nourishment as they eventually grow down from the top of the stone to the container of soil below.

To protect the plant and the soil smeared on the stone from sun and rain, a damp sheet of florist's green moss is wrapped around the entire stone and tied to it with twine. The plant is watered and sheltered carefully for a few weeks, and then gradually given more light and water as growth begins. By late September the roots will have grown down the rock and filled the pot below. Then the sheet of moss is removed and the soil washed from the rock gradually over a period of several weeks, beginning at the top and working down. As the last traces of soil are washed away, the beautiful thick roots are revealed clasping the stone as if they had grown there for centuries.

Of course, all these *ishi-tsuki* plants must have their branches pruned and shaped before they can truly be called bonsai. For it is not enough to pot and grow a plant well; it must be molded and cut, fashioned and trimmed, before it is a real bonsai.

Shaping and Pruning

F E W of the trees and shrubs we have grown thus far are so well formed that they need not be trimmed and trained before they can make good bonsai. And it is this technique that makes bonsai culture an art. For merely to stunt a tree by cutting it down or starving it is easy enough and ugly enough. But to produce a perfect miniature tree which will perhaps grow for hundreds of years without exceeding a foot or two in height, precisely proportioned in leaf, blossom, trunk, and twig—that is a difficult and wonderful art.

The true style of shaping bonsai leaves the trunk and branches clearly outlined, every part in perfect scale. Excess twigs are removed, revealing the main lines of the plant. Always the ideal form is kept in mind, that form which causes the observer to see far more than a small tree in a shallow pot—rather to see a towering and ancient pine with roots bared on the mountain side, a grove of quiet juniper, or a flaming autumn maple. Once this illusion is created, everything is done to keep it unchanged through the years.

Bonsai are shaped by pinching the tips of the new growth in spring and fall, by tying one branch to another, or by deftly bending and cutting. This shaping aims not so much at achieving symmetry, as at that rare beauty of balance hidden in seeming asymmetry. It does not force the plants into strange and unnatural shapes as was once the fashion. The tendency today is toward a picturesque simplicity such as one encounters everywhere in nature.

The best style for bonsai is nature's style; the best shape nature's shape. Bonsai growers must constantly study the way each tree grows in nature, and then try to capture these forms in their bonsai. Elms are upright and round-headed; cryptomeria columnar. To force these trees into strange and unnatural shapes is to violate not only the spirit of bonsai but the first rule of art: *The material defines the form.*

SHAPING

The Japanese sum up the qualities of a good bonsai with a simple phrase—*ichi-miki, ni-eda, san-nebari*: "first the trunk, second the branches, third the roots." These three things in perfect proportion make the true bonsai.

1. *Trunk.* The trunk is the basis of any form of tree, large or small. To be effective bonsai must have a trunk in good proportion to the branches, formed exactly as the trunk of mature specimens in nature. The trunk must taper gradually to the top. One that has been lopped off to reduce its height is rarely acceptable.

There was a time during the Tokugawa Era when bonsai makers delighted in creating very short, stout trunks out of all proportion to the branches. Or they bent them like the tentacles of an octopus in the so-called *tako-zukuri* style, or shaped them like a letter S. There were some who even tied the trunks of their bonsai in a loose knot like a pretzel. But such tortures are rarely practised today.

The modern bonsai has a trunk modeled exactly after its big brothers in the field. Elms are grown with straight, smooth trunks; seashore pines with leaning, wind-swept trunks. Even the decayed trunks of giant forest patriarchs are faithfully copied in the *saba-miki* style, where the greater part of the core is deliberately cut away leaving nothing but the outer shell.

From the earliest stages of development, plants for bonsai should be carefully selected and grown to develop the type of trunk desired. Seedlings and cuttings are often planted out in the ground for a year or two to develop thicker, more shapely trunks than they could make in pots. Proper training, straightening or bending, of the trunk while the plants are still young will prevent much needless labor and disappointment later.

2. *Branches and Leaves.* In times past the disposition of branches in bonsai was governed by laws as rigid as those in the art of flower arrangement. Branches emerging opposite each other on the trunk were frowned upon, and one branch or the other was removed to give alternate branching. Because plants were cultivated to be shown in the *tokonoma* or before a *byobu* or folding screen, they were grown with a right side and a wrong side from which to be viewed. To reduce their spread, branches were twisted like corkscrews or bent in the shape of a series of letter S's.

Fortunately, today, all that is required of any bonsai is that its branches be proportionate in length and thickness to the trunk. The branches are shaped naturally, so that they can be viewed from any side just as we enjoy trees in the field. The more neatly each branch is divided at the tips, the finer its twiggy growth, the more valuable it becomes. But all this does not mean that the branches are permitted to grow freely. They must be constantly thinned and pruned to keep them in bounds and to prevent them becoming so dense that they hide the beauty of the trunk.

One of the easiest ways to tell whether a bonsai has been well grown or not is to look at the tips of its branches. If an old tree looks old even to the tips or if a young tree displays a perfectly balanced network of twigs, that tree is well grown. To lend verisimilitude to weathered *saba-miki* bonsai, growers sometimes break off a branch or two close to the trunk, peel back the bark a bit and leave a ragged stump as if the branch had been hit by lightning or broken by accident.

Although the Japanese phrase does not mention leaves, foliage plays an important part in developing a perfect bonsai. Strangely enough, although the trunk and branches of a plant are quite drastically reduced in size by the dwarfing process, the foliage is scarcely changed at all. That is why it is so important to select small-leaved varieties at the start, or the foliage will always be out of proportion to the plant.

There are a few remedies for this disproportion when it occurs, however. In certain broad-leaved trees such as the maples, all the leaves are pinched off when they are practically mature in summer. This causes new leaves to form which are smaller and brighter in autumn color than they would be otherwise. In other cases, growing branches are cut back to dormant buds to cause them to sprout with late, small-leaved growths. These new growths may be pinched again if necessary, reducing them to one or two leaves, to give still later and smaller-leaved growths. Actually when-

ever very large broad-leaved trees are trained as bonsai, they
should be allowed only a few artistically shaped branches;
so that when the leaves appear, each leaf will, in essence,
take the place of a branch and thus make the plant seem
more in proportion.

Bonsai foliage is generally healthier, brighter, and neater
when the plants are kept in a sunny place and neither over-
watered nor overfed. But when the size of the leaves is still
disproportionate, thinning the leaves or old needles on a
tree will help relieve the feeling of heaviness somewhat.
Occasionally pine needles are shortened by being cut in half
when they are very long and untidy, but this like all the
other remedies is only a temporary expedient for what is,
after all, a persistent varietal fault. It is far better to choose
naturally small-leaved varieties and strains for bonsai from
the start.

3. *Roots.* Nothing encourages the illusion of great size
and age in bonsai more than the sight of a few heavy roots
exposed above ground, leaving the trunk of a plant and
entering the soil. Good rootage is one of the most important
factors in developing well-balanced bonsai. Without it
plants appear unstable, their trunks spring out of the
ground like telephone poles, they look top-heavy and unnatural. The best rootage is usually found in pot-grown
seedlings that have had their tap-roots cut short to develop
surface roots at an early age. Cuttings, layers, and trans-
plants from the field only develop good rootage after several
years of training in bonsai containers.

There are several ways to bare the crown of the plant and
expose the roots above the soil. However, it should be re-
membered that, if the roots are surfaced when the tree is
very young, they will rarely grow and thicken satisfactorily.

So it is best to let the roots get thick just under the surface and then expose them when they are well developed. The best time to expose the roots is when the plant is being potted. If it is being planted bare-root, the pliant roots may be arranged carefully in the container just as they are to appear, and then potted as usual. If the plant is being potted with a ball of soil about its roots, the ball is potted a bit higher than usual. Then as the plant is watered the soil about the crown and surface roots will be gradually washed away and the roots revealed.

When the surfaced roots are well developed on all sides of the trunk, are matched in size and perhaps interestingly branched, they are, of course, perfect. But when they all come from one side of the trunk and are poorly developed and spaced, they are called *kata-nebari*, or "one-sided root-age." The unstable picture they create may be offset by placing a stone at the base of the tree on the opposite side, or by mounding up the soil slightly and planting a ground cover over it. But this is makeshift. Bonsai plants should be grown and selected from the start with an eye to well-balanced, healthy root structure.

PRUNING

From the first day when collected plants are trimmed to compensate for loss of roots in digging, when seedlings and cuttings are pinched to induce bushy growth, when potted specimens are shaped to bring them into scale, pruning stands out as a vital part of bonsai culture. Indeed, the whole of Japanese gardening may be called a revelation in the art of pruning. For nowhere on earth have gardeners so cleverly used pruning shears to improve upon nature.

The curiously twisted appearance of Japanese pine trees

in gardens and temple grounds, for example, is achieved almost wholly by a method of pruning that gives relatively young trees a stunted and venerable appearance they would not otherwise attain in years. The leading shoot of each branch is cut back hard. The new growth coming out at right angles to the previous year's growth then gives the branch a new direction. The next year the tip is cut again and the new branch grows out in the opposite direction. This zig-zag process is carried out every year, excess branches are trimmed so that every line of the trunk is visible, and in time the tree assumes a stocky, gnarled appearance far beyond its years.

Bonsai are pruned in much the same way to reduce the size of branches, change their direction, to thin out dense growths that hide the line of trunk and roots, and to remove dead and diseased parts. Any of the styles described in Chapter IV could be achieved by skillful pruning alone, without the aid of wires or ties, bending or twisting. But the process is a long one calling for more skill and patience than most growers possess. So pruning is used more for holding plants within bounds, for shaping them roughly, and for keeping them well groomed after they have been given a finished form by wiring and tying.

Except for the usually drastic pruning given plants at the start to shape and head them back, most bonsai pruning is a constant process of nibbling. Each variety has its own time and method. The flowering apricot is pruned hard each year just after blooming, leaving only two growth buds on each branch. At the same time the flowering cherry is pruned very sparingly or not at all. Wisteria are pruned very hard each year in late winter, leaving only two growth buds on each branch, and sometimes again in August to

HOW TO SHAPE AND PRUNE BONSAI

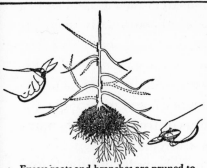

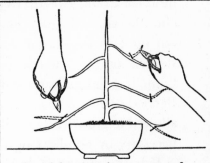

1. Excess roots and branches are pruned to shape the plant roughly and balance top growth with roots.

2. Remaining branches are pruned to change direction of growth and reduce size of the plant.

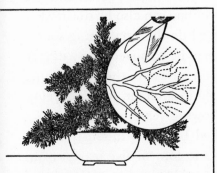

3. Matted, crossing twigs and branches are thinned to reveal main structure of bonsai.

4. Soft tip growths must be constantly pinched back to control growth and density.

5. New growth is pruned, thinned, or defoliated in summer to control size of plant and leaves. Needles are thinned or cut shorter.

6. Flower buds are thinned for artistic placement, fruit thinned to prevent death of plants from overbearing.

head back rank growth. Deciduous trees such as the maples, elms, beech, and zelkova are pinched continually throughout the growing season to develop a twiggy head, as every shoot is shortened to only one or two leaves again and again. Camellias and azaleas are pruned sparingly after blooming. Berried plants such as holly, hawthorn, and pyracantha are allowed to grow freely until flowers or fruit are set, then unnecessary or non-bearing twigs are removed.

If bushy growth is desired on crab apples, all the leaves on the current growth are removed in early summer to force side shoots, and these are then shortened in autumn to two or three growth buds. Bamboo can also be dwarfed at will by peeling off the sheaths while the very young shoots are just coming up; a sheath may be removed every day or less according to the hardness and growth of the young cane. If a nearly mature cane is topped in summer, it will develop beautiful dense foliage the following year.

Chrysanthemums are pinched back continuously on all lateral and sub-lateral branches to four or five leaves, from the time they are potted until mid-September. For dwarf or denser growth, conifers are pinched continuously from spring till autumn whenever unwanted growths appear. The soft young shoots are nipped off just as they begin to show new needles, leaving a bit at the base from which new growths will come. Weeping willows and tamarix that have had their new growth cut back to the base in late spring, will develop new weeping branches more slender and delicate than before.

The secret of successful bonsai culture lies in maintaining a constant balance between the top of a plant and its roots. Just as the roots are periodically pruned to fit a particular container, so the twigs and branches are pruned to fit the shape and size of tree we have in mind. The dwarfed plant which results is a product not only of root restriction but of this constant pruning process as well.

The interdependence of top growth and roots is greater than most growers realize. When roots are pruned heavily, new growth is stimulated above ground as well as below. Strong new branches appear on the tree which if allowed to grow will override and weaken the smaller, older branches that already give our tree its shape. So if the tree is to keep the form we have visualized for it, unwanted growths and errant twigs must be removed constantly.

There is only one rule of thumb that can be recommended in pruning bonsai: It is better to nip an unwanted branch in the bud today than cut it with shears tomorrow. If and when shears are used, the cuts should be made as neat and inconspicuous as possible.

WIRING AND BENDING

When bonsai cannot be readily shaped by pruning, several quick and easy methods of wiring and bending are employed to transform trunks and branches by force. Used with good judgment these mechanical devices can save much time and labor, but they are not a sure remedy for poor growing, bad taste, and impatience. In the hands of amateurs they too often become instruments of torture, as plants are trussed up in weird shapes that would make the "octopus" and "pretzel" bonsai makers of the Tokugawa Era blush. If there is one inviolable rule in wiring and shaping bonsai it is surely this: *Never bend or twist a stem or branch unnaturally.*

The most popular way to bend a branch or stem is to wind a wire around it spirally. Wiring is usually done when the plants are full of sap and pliant. Plants may be wired while they are still in the ground, in nursery tins or pots, or after they have established themselves in bonsai containers. For a few days before the operation they should be given less water to make them somewhat limp and easier to bend.

Soft copper wire annealed by holding it in a fire until glowing and then cooled in water is generally preferred, but common galvanized wire will serve as well. Indeed, there is some evidence that copper wire is toxic to some plants such as cherries and should not be used for them at all. The weight of the wire will vary from rather small gauge for tiny branches to very heavy gauge for strong trunks.

To begin wiring, one end of the wire is inserted deep in the soil near the base of the trunk to be trained. Then it is coiled firmly and evenly around the trunk rising at a 45 degree angle in ½- to 2-inch spirals, depending on the size and resistance of the trunk. If the bark is very tender, covered electrician's wire can be used instead of the bare annealed wire; or the trunk can first be wrapped with strips of paper, cloth, or raffia. At all costs the wire must not damage the bark or branches unduly.

When the wire is wound well beyond the area to be bent, the end should be cut off and tucked neatly out of the way. Then holding the wired trunk with both hands, slowly and gently force it into the desired position. If the wire selected is sufficiently stiff it will hold the bend in place by tension. In rare cases a second wire may be wound close to the first one for reinforcement. The same basic technique is used to wire the branches, only a lighter wire is used and its end is anchored by being wound around the trunk just below the branch instead of being inserted in the ground.

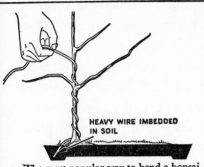

HEAVY WIRE IMBEDDED IN SOIL

1. The most popular way to bend a bonsai branch or stem is to wind a wire around it spirally.

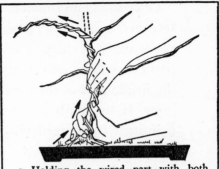

2. Holding the wired part with both hands, slowly and gently force it into the desired position.

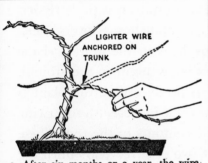

LIGHTER WIRE ANCHORED ON TRUNK

3. After six months or a year, the wire must be removed carefully or it will girdle and spoil the plant.

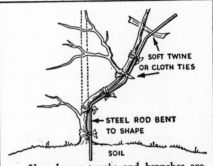

SOFT TWINE OR CLOTH TIES

STEEL ROD BENT TO SHAPE

SOIL

4. Very heavy trunks and branches are shaped by tying them to a steel rod bent in the desired form.

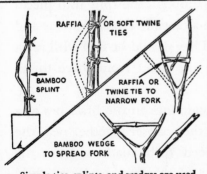

RAFFIA OR SOFT TWINE TIES

BAMBOO SPLINT

RAFFIA OR TWINE TIE TO NARROW FORK

BAMBOO WEDGE TO SPREAD FORK

5. Simple ties, splints, and wedges are used freely to train bonsai.

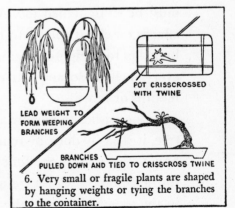

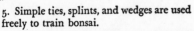

POT CRISSCROSSED WITH TWINE

LEAD WEIGHT TO FORM WEEPING BRANCHES

BRANCHES PULLED DOWN AND TIED TO CRISSCROSS TWINE

6. Very small or fragile plants are shaped by hanging weights or tying the branches to the container.

Once the bend is made, the trunk or branch must not be returned to its former position. When a sharp bend is made, particularly in thick limbs, the soft internal tissues on the part curved out are usually damaged; but similar tissues on the inside part of the curve are uninjured and continue to grow. If the limb is quickly straightened again these remaining tissues may be injured too and the branch or plant lost. It is always well to think twice and bend once.

After six months or a year, certainly before it begins to girdle the bark of the plant, the wire must be unwound and removed very carefully. If the branch has not become fixed in the interval it can be wired again until it is properly set.

To bend very heavy trunks or branches, growers sometimes insert a ⅜-inch steel rod bent in the desired shape beside the trunk of a plant in a large tub or in the ground. After making certain the rod is firmly seated, the plant is pulled down to it and tied every few inches with soft twine or strips of cloth, following the contours of the rod. These forms are left on the plant for two or three years until the trunk and branches assume the proper shape.

Of course, bonsai are not always bent; sometimes they must be straightened too. A bamboo cane split into pieces affords excellent splints to tie alongside crooked stems and branches to straighten them. They should be tied with raffia every inch or so and left on the plant from three to six months or more.

If one wishes to narrow a wide fork in the branches of a tree, it is easily done by tying them closer together near the base with raffia. If the fork needs to be made wider at the top, a bamboo stick is carefully whittled and wedged tightly in the crotch to spread the branches.

A rosewood stand 28 inches high holds a remarkable display of miniature bonsai. At the top, a cryptomeria and a holly fern *(Polystichum standishi)*. In the middle, a crab apple with twenty apples and a grove of Yezo spruce. At the bottom, a tiny St. Johnswort *(Hypericum senanense)* and a hornbeam *(Carpinus carpinoides)*.

The cascade chrysanthemum Ogurayama is grown here on a stone in *ishi-tsuki* style. Note the thick stem-like roots growing down into the container.

Branches are sometimes made to weep by hanging weights at their tips to pull them down. Or, better still, the bonsai pot is bound with twine, just as if it were a parcel for mailing, and the branches are pulled down and tied with string to these cross pieces of twine. These methods are often used to shape baby bonsai or fragile plants that are difficult to wire.

CODA

Actually there is much more to shaping bonsai than knowing how and when to trim or wire or bend. These facts are simply told. What is much more difficult is to convey the inner values, the feelings of this art. The bonsai maker is at once gardener, painter, and sculptor. His creation is alive and changing endlessly. These tiny boughs are filled with the pain and wonder of life. It is easy to see the rightness of what he does after it is done, but it is impossible to explain exactly how or why he does it.

As in all great works of art there is an inevitability of form in the best bonsai, an incontrovertible rightness, that gives us a sense of perfection and stability in a very imperfect and unstable world. That is why we turn to these tiny trees again and again for comfort and assurance, as we turn to great books, painting, or music. But as in all works of art there are many forms possible, and the beginner will ask— What is the perfect form for my bonsai? Part of the answer lies in the trees themselves, for we have seen that essentially the material defines the form. But the rest is that intangible seeking for inevitability that makes men give their lives to the endless trial and error that is art. That makes them put one word after another in a hundred rejected drafts, line after line in a thousand discarded sketches, note after note in ten thousand stricken measures until there emerges Shakespeare's *Hamlet,* da Vinci's *The Last Supper,* Beethoven's *Fifth Symphony.* It is this same quest for artistic perfection that leads the bonsai maker on.

Maintenance

CHAPTER X $\mathcal{N}$*O* matter how carefully plants for bonsai are selected, how cleverly prepared and potted, how skillfully pruned and shaped, they will not live and grow without constant care and maintenance. Bonsai are not for careless gardeners. One day without water, one month without light, one season without food can destroy a lifetime of work. The key to successful bonsai culture lies in the common everyday chores of watering, feeding, and grooming. Even the choicest bonsai is actually a product of many patient years of these simple, unassuming labors.

SHADE AND SHELTER

Bonsai have been grown on shelves and benches in country gardens, on roof tops and balconies of city apartments, even aboard Japanese merchant ships. But in all these places their requirements have been the same: plenty of sunshine, air, and water; a little protection from hot afternoon sun in midsummer and from freezing in midwinter; and the tender care of a bonsai lover. These plants do not have to be coddled. They can stand virtually the same conditions as their big brothers in the fields and forests, and they ask for little more.

The best place to keep established bonsai is on a table in an open corner of the garden, where they can get all the light and air they need. Only in the intense heat of summer will they sometimes need shading overhead. And then a very simple lath or reed screen can be put over them to break the strong afternoon sunlight. The rest of the year, especially in spring as the leaves and branches are developing, bonsai should have as much sun as possible to make strong, stocky growths. It is a serious mistake to keep bonsai too long in the home or under lath, glass, or trees. Bonsai are not indoor plants. They can be brought in for a few days to be enjoyed or protected, but their place is really outdoors in the open sun and air.

In winter, hardy evergreens such as the pines, juniper, spruce, yew, and cypress can take all the rain and cold the usual winter has to offer. But in very severe weather the containers sometimes break from the cold and the roots may be damaged. They can be protected by covering the pots with straw or some similar material, or by moving them indoors in the very worst weather. Of the conifers, only the cryptomeria and needle juniper need extraordinary winter protection for their delicate foliage, and should be given shelter when necessary. Japanese bonsai growers often erect a temporary bamboo or reed shelter over the bonsai bench enclosing it on the top and three sides. This light cover protects the plants from ice and snow which might break the tiny branches.

Most deciduous trees and shrubs can take considerable winter wind and cold. In fact the rigorous weather helps keep the trees from leafing out too soon in spring and growing too rank. Watering in winter should not be neglected for any bonsai, because dry winter air can be as damaging as cold. But it must be done before noon so that no excess water remains in the container at night to freeze the roots and break the pot.

Bamboo, wisteria, apricot, pomegranate, citrus, azaleas and other relatively tender plants are less tolerant of intense cold and must be given some winter protection to keep their soil from freezing. They may be put in a coldframe, porch, or cool glasshouse at night and brought out again during the day to get sun and water. Bog plants, reeds, and rushes grown in basins of water should be kept in the house in freezing weather.

Except for those special plants such as the apricot, forsythia, and winter-blooming jasmine which are forced into bloom for the New Year season, bonsai should never be kept in a heated room or greenhouse during winter. For if the plants are suddenly exposed to high temperatures they will send out premature growths that are weak and sickly, and the normal balance of the plant will be seriously upset.

WATERING BONSAI

The technique of watering bonsai depends entirely on the nature of the plant's root system, its age, location, and the season of the year. Bonsai must be soaked thoroughly after potting or repotting to settle the roots and soil in the container. The fresh soil will absorb a great deal of water at this time without injury to the plant. But for the first few weeks after planting, the original soil ball will dry out more rapidly than the new soil around it because it is full of roots. To prevent wilting it will be necessary to water the plant carefully at first until enough roots grow out into the new soil to keep the plant adequately supplied with moisture. From then on watering will become more frequent as the plants grow more and more pot-bound.

Bonsai grow best when a uniform amount of water is always present in the soil. This can be achieved by watering the plants heavily at infrequent intervals, by keeping the soil neither too wet nor too dry. The soil should be allowed to become half dry, then as the plants are watered heavily the water pushes out the carbon dioxide accumulated in the soil, and as it drains away new air enters the soil from above. In this way roots grow evenly throughout the pot and an occasional drying of the upper crust causes no harm. But frequent sprinklings that wet only the upper crust fail to aerate the soil at all and attract the roots to the surface where they are easily killed by a sudden drought.

It is impossible to say how often bonsai must be watered. That depends entirely on the soil used, the weather, the location of the plant, its size and stage of growth. In the wet season or for newly potted plants it may be only once or twice a week; in summer or with baby bonsai it may be from one to five times a day. But from spring to early summer when plants are growing vigorously, all bonsai should be watered less. Too much moisture and food at this season stimulates rank growth that may destroy the shape and balance of the plant, and even prevent it from flowering and fruiting normally. At this season, it is better to let the plants almost reach the wilting point each time before watering them.

Bonsai should always be watered by hand using a sprin-

kling can with a very fine spray. Watering with a hose
sprayer or even a can with a coarse nozzle is likely to wash
the soil out of the pots and quickly ruin the plants. If the
water to be used is first allowed to stand in a clean tub or
barrel for a few days, it will settle in temperature and re-
lease any chlorine or chemicals that have been added to it.
Rain or well water is always preferable to tap water, especially where the latter is very alkaline or highly treated. The
water should be applied very gently to the pots, two or three
times in succession until the soil is saturated and the excess
runs freely from the drainage hole below. If the pots are
properly drained they cannot be harmed by this heavy
watering any more than by several days of rainfall. Indeed,
pots of bald cypress, beech, wisteria, birch, and other
water-loving plants are sometimes set in shallow trays of
water in the hot, dry summer months to keep them properly
wet. But, as a rule, bonsai must drain perfectly at all times,
or else the plants should be repotted as soon as possible to
prevent them from becoming waterlogged.

Washing the foliage of bonsai occasionally with a fine
spray of water is almost as important as watering the roots.
Especially in cities blighted by soot and smog, this foliage
bath keeps the leaves free of dust, controls red spider and
aphids, and helps the plants look fresher and greener. It is
best to spray the plants early in the morning or evening to
avoid possible scalding or spotting of the leaves in the mid-
day sun. But this sprinkling must never be confused with
the regular process of watering. It is primarily intended for
the foliage and not the roots of the plants.

FEEDING BONSAI

Because we are trying to grow the finest possible plant in the least amount of soil, bonsai must be fed regularly to replace the nutrients leached out of the soil by frequent watering and hungry roots. While newly planted bonsai can go many months or even a year without feeding, they must sooner or later be given nourishment or they will weaken and die. But bonsai must never be fed until they are established in their pots. Nor should they be fed when they are sick or dry. Too much food is worse than no food at all; food at the wrong time may upset the balance of the plant completely.

The Japanese use a wide variety of fertilizers for bonsai, according to the season, kind of plant, and specific results desired. Soy-bean, cotton-seed, or rape-seed meal; blood, fish, or bone meal; and bird and animal manures are some of the more popular natural fertilizers. Inorganic or chemical plant foods are never used for bonsai because they are too strong and quick-acting and might easily burn the roots.

The organic or natural fertilizers are applied in several ways. Perhaps the most effective are the liquid fertilizers, made by soaking one part of the meals or manures with ten parts water in a covered tub or barrel for several weeks. The mixture is stirred frequently and when it is thoroughly putrid, the clear stock at the top is diluted with about thirty parts water and applied to the plants. Another popular method is to make a paste of rape-seed, soy-bean, or fish meal by letting the meal stand in a closed jar with a small amount of water for several days. The resulting paste is rolled into balls about ½-inch in diameter, and three or four of these are placed on top the soil at the corners of

HOW TO MAINTAIN BONSAI

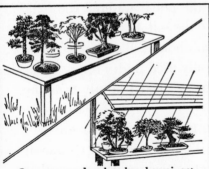

1. On open garden benches bonsai get plenty of sunshine, air, and water, with some shading in midsummer.

2. Wraps, a cold frame, or light shelter over the bench gives protection from winter winds, snow, and rain.

3. Bonsai must be watered gently but thoroughly according to the season and needs of each plant.

4. Spraying bonsai overhead with a mist of water keeps them healthy and pest free.

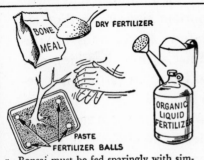

BONE MEAL

DRY FERTILIZER

ORGANIC LIQUID FERTILIZER

PASTE
FERTILIZER BALLS

5. Bonsai must be fed sparingly with simple organic fertilizers, but never when dry or sick, newly planted or growing too vigorously.

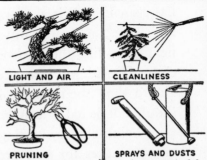

LIGHT AND AIR

CLEANLINESS

PRUNING

SPRAYS AND DUSTS

6. Cleanliness, light, and air are powerful remedies for most bonsai ills. Sprays and dusts cannot always cure careless growing.

each medium-sized pot. When the pot is watered the balls disintegrate slowly and sink into the soil. Fertilizers in paste form are always used for *ishi-tsuki* bonsai. Blood meal, bone meal, and wood ashes are generally used in dry form, either placed in the corners of the pot or dusted lightly over the surface.

Needless to say, plants recently potted in fresh soil will not need food for some time. The limited area in bonsai pots magnifies the harmful effects of overfertilizing, so that food must be given sparingly and only when needed. Always make sure that the soil is moist before feeding, and water thoroughly immediately after applying dry or paste fertilizers to prevent burning the roots. It is always better to give a little food often than a great deal at once. Fertilizers should never be placed on the trunk, leaves, or branches.

The time and amount of feeding vary according to the plant, its location, and the grower's experience. Conifers are fed very sparingly in spring and summer, with the exception of young plants still being shaped, because feeding during the growing season encourages soft, rank growths. The best season for feeding conifers is autumn, after growth has ceased. This is also an important time for feeding all fruit trees, and all plants that form flower buds for the next year—like the apricot, quince, winter jasmines, and cherry. Deciduous trees are also fed again just as they begin to shed their leaves. As a general rule, most plants should not be fed as heavily in spring as they are later in the year, because heavy feeding added to the impetus of spring growth makes for very gross branches and foliage, sometimes at the expense of flowers and fruit. It is better to encourage moderate spring growth and feed the plants later as the leaves and branches mature. Flowering plants like the chrysanthemum, however, are fed regularly from the time growth begins until flower buds are formed; then all feeding is stopped until the next growing season.

Most plants welcome several moderate feedings in early spring, summer, and autumn. Acid-loving plants such as camellias, azaleas, and rhododendrons should be given soybean or cotton-seed meal. Fruit trees such as the persimmon, pear, apple, and citrus appreciate fertilizers with a high phosphoric acid content like bone meal. Strong, leafy plants that need much nitrogen to stay green will require blood and fish meal occasionally.

It is impossible to be dogmatic about feeding bonsai; there are no schedules or formulas. One can only watch his plants for signs of hunger and anticipate seasonal needs. Bonsai are not fed as other plants to force larger growths, flowers, and fruit; but simply to keep them active and healthy, vigorous but small. Our feeding must be regulated to keep the *status quo*, not destroy it.

PESTS AND DISEASES

Bonsai are, of course, attacked by the same pests and diseases as their big brothers in nature. But because these plants are reduced in size and growth any affliction is magnified and urgent.

As with any problem, the best remedy is prevention. Buying healthy, vigorous stock; planting and spacing carefully; providing constant cleanliness, light, and air are the most effective ways of meeting any pest or disease.

Aphids and scale, for example, can be discouraged by simply controlling ants in the growing area. Placing the legs of the bonsai table in wide crocks of water treated with a powerful insecticide will curb ants and other climbing insects. Frequent spraying of the foliage with water will take care of red spider and aphids. Slugs and snails are easily controlled by poison baits; caterpillars and worms by hand picking.

When chemical sprays are used on bonsai it is important that the soil in the pots is moist, and the weather is cool and cloudy to prevent burning. Oil emulsions such as Volck will control scale if applied just as the young scales are hatched in spring. Grasshoppers, beetles, and other chewing pests may be controlled by spraying stomach poisons such as lead arsenate on the new foliage. Fungus diseases are cleared up by spraying with Bordeaux, Fermate, or other fungicides. But in the last analysis the best remedies are cleanliness, light, and air. Chemical sprays and dusts cannot cure careless growing.

Unless one is deliberately careless, bonsai will not die easily. Ten generations have marveled at the timeless wonder of a single tiny tree. There are many specimens a hundred, two hundred, even three hundred years old. No other potted plant grows old so gracefully, increasing in beauty and value with the years. Indeed, bonsai are a permanent investment in beauty, a priceless heritage, a living bit of immortality.

Index